"Imagine a one-on-one conversation with a communication guru, mentoring, modeling, and motivating you to become a more effective and efficient communicator. You need not imagine, because that guru, Kenneth Davis, has provided those three *Ms* in *The McGraw-Hill 36-Hour Course in Business Writing and Communication*, a book that will transform your hope and dreams for improving your writing into the reality of becoming a better writer."

DR. LYLE SUSSMAN
Professor and Chairman, Department of
Management and Entrepreneurship
College of Business
University of Louisville
Coauthor of *Smart Moves, Smart Moves for People in Charge,
What to Say to Get What You Want, Yes You Can,
Close the Deal,* and *Lost and Found*

THE ———
McGRAW-HILL
36-Hour Course

BUSINESS
WRITING AND
COMMUNICATION

SECOND EDITION

Kenneth W. Davis, Ph.D.

Mc Graw Hill

New York Chicago San Francisco Lisbon London Madrid Mexico City
Milan New Delhi San Juan Seoul Singapore Sydney Toronto

The **McGraw·Hill** Companies

1 2 3 4 5 6 7 8 9 10 11 12 13 14 15   WFR/WFR   1 9 8 7 6 5 4 3 2 1 0

ISBN 978-0-07-173826-2
MHID   0-07-173826-6

McGraw-Hill books are available at special quantity discounts to use as premiums and sales promotions or for use in corporate training programs. To contact a representative, please e-mail us at bulksales@cgraw-hill.com.

To my fellow members of the Association of Professional Communication Consultants, especially Dan Dieterich, Lee Clark Johns, and Barbara Shwom

CONTENTS

ACKNOWLEDGMENTS

For making this edition possible, I thank:

- The readers of, and commentors on, my blog at manageyour writing.com, including Mohammed Al-Taee, Adam Freedman, Danielle Ingram, Roy Jacobsen, Delaney Kirk, Norm Leigh, David William Peace, Dwayne Phillips, Brad Shorr, Cheryl Stephens, Matthew Stibbe, Raymond P. Ward, and Joanna Young
- My designer, Dean Eller, of DesignMark, Inc., Indianapolis, Indiana
- My agent, Paul S. Levine
- My team at McGraw-Hill, including Michele Wells, Nancy Hall, and Alison Shurtz
- Above all, my wife and partner, Bette Davis

INTRODUCTION: MANAGE YOUR WRITING

I n this knowledge economy, writing is the chief value-producing activity. But you may not be writing as well as you could. That may be because you think writing requires a special talent that some people have and some people don't.

In fact, writing is a process that can be managed like any other business process. If you can manage people, money, or time, then you can manage your writing. And you can profit from the results.

This book will give you the tools to become—in the next 36 hours— a more effective, efficient manager of your own writing.

- You'll become more *effective* because you'll learn to produce writing that gets things done.
- You'll become more *efficient* because you'll learn to produce more effective writing in less time.

How can this magic happen in just 36 hours? It'll happen because you'll learn to take the management skills you already have and apply them to the process of writing. Remember, whether or not the word *manager* is part of your job title, you clearly are a successful manager. Otherwise, you wouldn't have

- the money to buy this book,
- the position to have somebody else buy it for you,
- or the time and initiative to be browsing through it in a bookstore.

Through your experience in business and in life, you've learned to *manage*: to manage people, to manage money, to manage time. This book will teach you how to use these same skills when you write.

Let me tell you a story. When I was a kid growing up in rural Iowa, there was a local fisherman who had more money than common sense. He always had the newest, most expensive fishing gear, but he didn't always know how to use it.

One fall he decided to take up ice fishing. He ordered the very best cold-weather clothing, the very best portable shelter, the very best ice saw and tackle. The first winter day our local reservoir had frozen over enough, he was out on the ice at dawn. He set up his shelter, sawed his hole in the ice, sat on his new folding stool, and waited.

Three hours passed without even a sign of a fish. The disgusted fisherman was about to call it quits and head home when he saw a teen-age kid in faded blue jeans and a faded green Army field jacket head out onto the ice. The kid whacked a hole in the ice with a hammer, baited a hook, and immediately pulled out a nice fish. Within 10 minutes, the kid had a bucketful and turned back for the shore.

The older man yelled for him, but the kid was apparently out of voice range. So the man started walking fast toward him and finally caught up with him at the shore.

"Son," the man said, "I've been out here three hours without catching a fish, and you've pulled out half a dozen in 10 minutes. What's your secret?"

"Hmrm hmrm," the boy muttered.

"What's that?" asked the man.

"HMRM HMRM," answered the boy, louder.

"I'm sorry, son; I can't understand you. What's your secret?"

The boy moved his hand to his face, took a handful of something out of his mouth, and explained.

"WARM WORMS."

Well, OK, that story didn't really happen. But I wanted you to believe, for a while, that it *had* happened in order to make two points:

1. Writing can change and even create reality. For a while, my words made that story real for you. And the writing you do on the job can create a new, better reality for you in your work life. On his blog, my favorite management guru, Tom Peters, quoted novelist James Baldwin that "you write in order to change the world." Tom continued, "Call me hopelessly naïve, but I believe there is no excuse for any variety of 'business writing' that should be crafted any less carefully or aim any less high than a great novel or great inaugural address. After all, we do aim—day in and day out—to change the world via our human collectivities called enterprises. Right?"
2. This will be a "warm worms" book. It will give you practical, down-to-earth tools—the equivalent of a hammer, a bucket, and a mouthful of night crawlers—to re-create yourself as a more effective, efficient writer.

BE YOUR OWN COMMUNICATION DEPARTMENT

A *New Yorker* cartoon shows a tiny newsstand with a big sign. "Fred's Newsstand—," it reads, "Forefront of the New Post-Industrial Information Society."

We're all Fred, of course. The information society is a fact, and it affects the work every one of us does, from building cars to selling newspapers. As futurist John Naisbitt wrote, "The information society is an economic reality, not an intellectual abstraction." Yet most of us haven't learned the skills we need to survive and thrive in this new knowledge economy.

This fact is particularly important because more and more of us—me included—are entrepreneurs and "intrapreneurs." For the small business owner—or for the owner of "You, Inc.," within a large business—the upside of the knowledge economy is the fact that the creation or communication of knowledge does not require a large organization; the lone David can compete effectively with the Goliath. For example, some of the computer programming for a London cab company was done by a solo entrepreneur working from his Indiana farmhouse. The downside, however, is that the same standard of communication excellence is expected from a one- or two-person operation as from a giant corporation with its own communication department.

As revolutionary marketer Seth Godin has pointed out, much writing now goes to its readers "unfiltered," without an editor working on it first. He continued, "The thing most people miss most is that they no longer have an excuse. Without a publisher/editor/boss to blame, your writing is your writing."

So how do you compete? By being your own communication department.

Begin by understanding the times we live in. One of the most perceptive commentators on the knowledge economy is Alvin Toffler, whose book *The Third Wave* outlines three times of major change in human activity:

1. The first of these "waves," said Toffler, came several thousand years ago when hunting and fishing were replaced by farming as humanity's main work. In the resulting agricultural economy, wealth consisted chiefly of the ownership of land.

2. The second wave happened only about 150 to 200 years ago, when farming was replaced by manufacturing as our major economic activity, at least in the Western world. (That revolution—the industrial revolution—was not a bloodless one: the U.S. Civil War was, to some extent, a conflict between a largely agricultural South and an increasingly industrialized North.) In the resulting industrial economy, wealth consisted chiefly of the ownership of factories.

3. Now, said Toffler, a third wave is sweeping over us. Manufacturing has been giving way rapidly to the processing of information

as humanity's major economic activity. As we have entered the information or knowledge economy, wealth has come to consist of the ownership of information—or rather, the ability to collect and communicate information. James Champy was right when he wrote in his book *Reengineering Management,* "Knowledge is power, as the cliché has it. But knowledge is not easy to come by. You earn it by thinking. And all we have to think about is information. So make sure that the information 'gets around.'"

Even as early as the late 1980s, Tom Peters was finding striking examples of the wealth that lies in communicating information. Peters reported that the little publication called *The Official Airline Guide*—a for-sale compilation of schedule information (information that the airlines gave away free)—sold in 1988 for $750 million, three times the selling price of Ozark Airlines that same year.

In other words, the right formula for collecting and communicating free airline information was worth more than all the planes, equipment, and other assets of an airline itself.

If collecting and communicating information is our main work for today and tomorrow, we'd better get good at it. In a knowledge economy, our personal success and the success of our organizations depend on this "knowledge work." Management guru Peter Drucker, writing in *Managing in the Next Century,* put it this way: "Physical resources no longer provide much of an advantage, nor does skill. Only the productivity of knowledge workers makes a measurable difference."

Unfortunately, however, most of us are not very good at communicating our knowledge, and the results can be disastrous. W. Edwards Deming, the twentieth century's leading advocate for "quality" as a business goal, estimated that "85 percent of failures in quality are failures in communication." A big part of the problem is the way we think about communication. Too often we make third-wave communication decisions as if we were still living in a first- or second-wave society.

In first- and second-wave societies, communication often was one-way, top-down. Information was held at the very top of organizational pyramids and passed down to workers only as needed. Most of the time, most people—whether they worked in a field or in a factory—needed to be only passive receivers of communication.

Moreover, in first- and second-wave societies, communication communities were small and uniform. A first-wave farmer may have communicated with only a few hundred people in a lifetime, all people very much like himself. A second-wave plant manager communicated with more people, but that manager probably saw them as interchangeable.

In their book, *Thinking for a Living*, Ray Marshall and Marc Tucker pointed out that our educational system has not yet caught up with the communication needs of a knowledge economy. "Schools' curriculum and methods," they wrote, "are matched to the needs of a half-century ago, rather than to today's requirements. Fifty years ago, relatively few students needed sophisticated communications skills, so students were not required to write much and teachers were not asked to spend much time working with them to improve what they wrote. Students are still not required to write much and teachers are given very little time to help them improve their writing."

In third-wave organizations, pyramids have been flattened or dissolved, and valuable knowledge lives everywhere. All members of the organization have to be not only consumers of communication but also producers of it. *Everybody* in a third-wave organization has to be a skilled communicator. As marketing wizard Harry Beckwith wrote in *The Invisible Touch*, "Communication is not a skill. It is *the* skill." And "perhaps the most important lesson from the Iraq war," wrote David Newkirk and Stuart Crainer, "is that managing real-time communications is as important as managing real-time processes. Communication is moving from being a peripheral, specialist responsibility to being an essential and integral element of corporate leadership." Similarly, central to all five recommendations of the 9/11 Commission was the need for improved communication.

In addition, a third-wave knowledge worker may well communicate with tens of thousands of people from diverse backgrounds around the world. This diverse audience makes communication much more complex, demanding greater flexibility and sensitivity.

In the knowledge economy, the benefits of improved communication are many. In the insurance industry, for example, the cover letter from the agent, the "producer," to the underwriter is crucial. As Robert Goldstone, vice president and medical director at Pacific Mutual Life, has written, "A good cover letter may save your case." *Forbes* magazine has reported that "at AMEC Offshore, the big British engineering and construction firm, the cost of piping offshore oil platforms dropped 15 percent after intensive work on communications skills." The Families and Work Institute found that "the number one factor employees say will convince them to accept a job offer" is "open communication." And a Watson Wyatt study comparing financially high-performing companies with their lower-performing competitors found that

- "Communications professionals in high-performing organizations play a strategic role."
- "High-performing organizations do a better job of explaining change."
- "High-performing organizations focus on communicating with and educating their employees."
- "High-performing organizations provide channels for upward communication."
- "Employees in high-performing organizations have a better understanding of organizational goals and their part in achieving them."

So if you're sold by now—if you're committed to becoming a more effective third-wave communicator—what (besides taking this course) can you do? Here are a few suggestions:

1. Pay attention to the communication you're part of in a typical week. Think about how many messages you receive and send. Consider ways you could help yourself or others by communicating more effectively.

2. Pay special attention to the actual results of your speaking and writing. Figure out what communication strategies work for you and what strategies don't. Notice when you're understood and when you aren't. "There is one thing worse than not communicating," said educational theorist Edgar Dale. "It is thinking you have communicated when you have not."

3. Read and listen to communication from cultures and countries other than your own. In Appendix B of this book you'll learn an approach to communicating across cultures. Meanwhile, however, pick up occasional issues of unfamiliar magazines. Spend a few minutes with a cable channel from another culture or subculture. With each exposure, you'll learn new communication techniques.

4. Make sure that your communication process is as efficient and effective as possible. This is what this book is about, of course—streamlining and supercharging your writing process.

5. Start collecting tools—methods and techniques for effective communication. You'll find some especially powerful tools in this book. Also start your own "steal" file of effective speaking and writing that you receive. If you get a particularly good direct-mail letter, save it. If you hear a particularly powerful sales presentation, take notes about what's making it so powerful. You'll soon have a useful toolbox of ideas and models.

In short, begin to realize that communication is an important part of whatever work you do. Begin to think of yourself as a third-wave communicator. If you do, you'll be your own communication department.

WRITING IN A KNOWLEDGE ECONOMY

Did you, by any chance, stop to question the first sentence in this introduction? "In this knowledge economy," it claimed, "writing is the chief value-producing activity." This is a pretty big claim—especially when many people think of writing as a skill that's perhaps *nice* to have but by no means "real work." My former Indiana University colleague, Bobby Knight, spoke for many people when he said, "All of us learn to write in the second grade. Most of us then go on to greater things."

I can't be too critical of Coach Knight. (I wouldn't dare.) Even people who saw the knowledge economy coming, and who realized that knowledge requires communication for it to pay off, didn't always foresee how much of that communication would be in writing.

After all, many messages that a hundred years ago would have been put into writing are now transmitted orally by telephone wire and satellite relay. "Why write a letter," I've been asked, "when you can pick up a telephone?"

This question is an important one. To be sure, oral communication has a bunch of advantages:

- First, it can be instantaneous; the moment you decide to say something, you can say it.
- Moreover, oral communication, especially when it is face to face, can carry far more information than just words can express. A rising pitch or a raised eyebrow can convey shades of meaning not possible on the written page.
- Perhaps most important, oral messages can be answered with immediate feedback, even during the message. You can constantly adjust your communication based on your listener's response.
- Speaking, in short, is fast, easy, and efficient.

Writing, in contrast, is almost always slower and more difficult. This is partly because we have much less practice at it. And in a business, writing is expensive, requiring equipment and materials. In addition, the written word, for most of the history of business, has been slow to move, taking hours and days to get from one office, one city, or one nation to another. For all these reasons, the invention of the telephone was very good news for business. During the late nineteenth century and most of the twentieth century, the proportion of business communication put in writing almost surely went down.

But oral communication has its disadvantages, too:

- The main one is impermanence. Speech disappears as soon as it's uttered; that's why an oral contract is "not worth the paper it's written on." Speech can, of course, be recorded, but much of its important content doesn't survive the recording process.
- And even if speech is recorded on tape or disc, its content is extraordinarily difficult to search and retrieve. Try finding every mention of Microsoft in an audio or video recording of a two-day meeting. Hint: it will take you two days.

Writing, on the other hand, is forever. A written communication can last as long as the material on which it's inscribed, and it is always available for rechecking. In fact, that's why writing was invented—and for "business" purposes at that. When humanity experienced Toffler's "first wave," moving from hunting and gathering to agriculture, the first writing began to appear, in the form of warehouse inventories and other business documents, on clay tablets. These ancient pieces of business writing are still being found throughout the Middle East.

In her book *Doing Business*, Olivia Vlahos quoted from one of these documents, a clay tablet sent from creditors in the city of Assur, in modern Iraq, to a debtor at the end of a caravan route in modern Turkey: "Thirty years ago you left the city of Assur. You have never made a deposit since, and we have not recovered one shekel of silver from you, but we have never made you feel bad about this. Our tablets have been going to you with caravan after caravan, but no report from you has ever come here. . . . Please do come back right away or deposit the silver for us. If not, we will send you a notice from the local ruler and the police, and thus put you to shame in the assembly of merchants. You will also cease to be one of us."

As Vlahos said, "the modern debt collector would be hard put to better that communication."

The relative permanence of writing also lets it be used to "freeze" oral discussion. My friend Lee Woods, who worked as a writer at Resort Condominiums International, said that writing was often used there "to give closure, to record agreement." And Terry Pearce, in his acclaimed book *Leading Out Loud*, pointed out the importance of writing as a way of "disciplining your voice" in preparation for oral communication. "Writing," he says, "reveals fuzzy thinking, exposes slurred distinctions: it clarifies."

In addition to its permanence, written communication has the advantage of being easily skimmed or indexed so that a reader can find exactly that part of the message that she needs. For this reason, most digital audio and video recordings are now accompanied by "written" metainformation: the index of tracks on an audio CD or "chapters" on a DVD, for example. Some CD-ROM products index, in "writing," audio or video material down to the level of individual words, so that you can, in fact, find every time the word *Microsoft* was spoken during a two-day meeting.

Moreover, the old gap between speech and writing in speed and cost has pretty much closed. Computers, networks, and satellite data transmission have made a written message as cheap and fast as a phone call, while keeping all the advantages of written words. In addition, the globalization of business, requiring communication across many time zones, has made phone conversations potentially inconvenient.

As a result, the century-long trend toward spoken communication has reversed. More and more business communication is being conducted in writing. E-mail and Web pages are, after all, written documents produced to be read. A 2000 study by the Poynter Institute found that readers of online news sites look first at the *text*—a very different way of reading than in print media, where readers tend to look first at graphics. On the Web, only 22 percent of users look at graphics first.

In summary, Steve Rubel, on his blog Micro Persuasion, wrote that the "digital age has dramatically upped the ante [for] one skill above all—good writing." He continued, "Almost every white-collar job today requires good communication skills. There's nothing new to report there.

However, what is new is that much of the way we communicate today in business is in writing through email. So even if you're not a scribe by trade, you're still a writer by default. Writing not your forte? That was just fine 10 years ago, but not anymore. Writing is how business gets done."

WHAT A WRITING COURSE CAN— AND CAN'T—DO

Now for a confession—one I've never seen in any other business writing book: books and courses about writing can't teach you everything you need to be an effective writer. That's the bad news. But here's the good news: what this book can't teach, you almost certainly already know.

You see, writing requires two abilities. Only one can be taught. If you have the first ability, this book can teach you the second.

The first ability, the one that can't be taught, is what writing teacher and researcher Stephen Krashen called "competence." Competence is our deep, unconscious knowledge of language. We acquire competence in spoken language by hearing it over and over again. We learn how a language *sounds*.

For example, can you state the rule in the English language for the order of adjectives of number, age, and nationality? You probably didn't even know there *was* such a rule; you and I certainly weren't taught it in school. Nevertheless, you know the rule perfectly. You know to say "two old Japanese accountants," not "old two Japanese accountants" or "Japanese two old accountants." This rule—not really a *rule* but a practice—is part of your competence in English, learned unconsciously from hearing and reading hundreds of thousands of sentences in which this practice was followed.

The English language has tens or hundreds of thousands of such practices, only a few of which ever get taught formally in classrooms and training rooms. Many of these practices—including the example in the last paragraph—apply both in speaking and in writing. Many others, however, apply only in written English. Writing demands an explicitness, a clarity, a degree of organization that speaking does not, and so it requires additional competence. We learn such competence through reading. We learn how writing "sounds."

This reading doesn't have to be great literature. *Sports Illustrated, Scientific American,* or a Danielle Steel novel will serve as well as Shakespeare. The only requirements are that there be a lot of it and that it be self-motivated. If reading is going to produce writing competence, it must be *transparent.* That is, the reader must be paying attention not to the words and sentences themselves but to what they say.

By the time you're reading this book, you almost surely have the competence you need to be an effective business writer. But don't stop. To continue to grow as a writer, you need to continue to grow as a reader. As the American novelist William Faulkner said, "Read, read, read. Read everything—trash, classics, good and bad, and see how they do it. Just like a carpenter who works as an apprentice and studies the master. Read! You'll absorb it. Then write."

What teaching or training *can* do is take writers who already have competence and give them a second ability, an ability that Krashen called "performance." Performance is the ability to actually produce language. Performance always lags behind competence. Any parent knows that children have competence in spoken language (they can understand it) long before they acquire performance (and start talking).

Almost any child will soon learn to translate his competence into spoken performance. But performance in writing is harder to get. That's where teaching and training come in. For adults, training (like the course in this book) can give those who already have competence in written English three important components of performance:

1. Confidence

The first thing training can give you is *confidence.* One of the main reasons that the writing performance of most adults doesn't match their competence is that they lack confidence in their ability to write. They are consciously or unconsciously afraid of failing. *Writer's block* is perhaps the most familiar symptom of this lack of confidence.

So this book, like all good writing training, is attitude-based. It will help you to realize the competence you already have and remind you that writing is much more than just following rules. As the beginning of this introduction said, this book will stress the fact that writing well is not a talent that you are either born with or not; it's a business activity you can manage like any other business activity.

2. Process Knowledge

The second thing you can get from training is *process knowledge*. The knowledge about writing that comes from extensive reading is all *product* knowledge. Just as you can drive cars for years without having any idea about the automobile manufacturing process, you can read books and articles for years without having any idea about the writing process— the false starts, stumbles, and revisions that writers have to go through. For example, you'd never know that I've revised this paragraph at least a dozen times. Jonathan Swift, author of *Gulliver's Travels*, described the writing process this way:

> Blot out, correct, insert, refine,
> Enlarge, diminish, interline;
> Be mindful, when invention fails,
> To scratch your head, and bite your nails.

Therefore, this book, like all good writing training, is *process*-oriented. Rather than focusing on details of written products, such as clauses and colons, it focuses on the *steps* good writers go through, the decisions they make. Again, W. Edwards Deming, the "quality" guy, wrote, "If you can't describe what you are doing as a process, you don't know what you're doing."

That's why the best writing teachers and trainers are also working writers, "walking their talk."

3. Reinforcement

The third component that training can provide is ongoing *reinforcement*. Some of this reinforcement can be in the form of *reminders* of the confidence and process knowledge that good writers have learned. Some can be in the form of *feedback*, responses to work in progress.

This book offers four opportunities for reinforcement:

1. Most chapters have exercises for you to do and then compare your answers with mine.
2. The book ends with an exam leading to a certificate of completion.
3. The book includes lots of advice on how to evaluate yourself and how to learn from the feedback you get on your on-the-job writing.
4. You can go to my website, manageyourwriting.com, for tips that will give ongoing reinforcement of what you've learned in this book.

The three components of effective writing training—confidence, process knowledge, and reinforcement—are interdependent.

As you become more confident, you'll become more receptive to new process knowledge and more comfortable seeking and receiving feedback about your writing. As you gain more process knowledge, you'll become more confident about your writing process and more skillful at receiving reinforcement. And as you receive (and give) ongoing reinforcement, both your confidence and your process knowledge will grow.

Training in writing can't do everything. But with the competence you already have, this book can make you more confident and knowledgeable—and thus more efficient and effective. And it can make you a lifelong learner of writing, getting better and better each day, week, month, and year.

HOW TO USE THIS BOOK

This book has 12 chapters, or lessons, each covering a step in an effective writing process.

As I've mentioned, most chapters have exercises to complete. Most also ask you to apply what you've learned in that chapter to the very next piece of on-the-job writing you do and evaluate the result. Including exercises, on-the-job applications, and self-evaluations, the 12 chapters should take you an average of three hours each to complete. As the title says, this book is a 36-hour course.

This book also includes four appendixes:

- Appendix A, "Manage Your Online Writing," deals with special considerations for writing for online reading: e-mail, Web pages, blogs, and the like.
- Appendix B, "Manage Your Global Writing," gives you some special tools to use when you write internationally.
- Appendix C, "Manage Your Speaking," tells you how to use what you've learned in this book when you make oral presentations.
- Appendix D, "Resources for Managing Your Writing," lists further tools.

As you work through this book and after you've finished, please feel free to e-mail me at ken@manageyourwriting.com and to visit my website at manageyourwriting.com.

Let me repeat what you've read earlier:

In this knowledge economy, writing is the chief value-producing activity. But you may not be writing as well as you could. Perhaps you think writing requires a special talent that some people have and some people don't.

In fact, writing is a process that can be managed like any other business process. If you can manage people, money, or time, then you can manage your writing. And you can profit from the results.

"THE DISCIPLINE OF THE CRAFT"

In a cartoon I saw once, a Hollywood producer bellows to his secretary, "I want to send a memo to the parking-lot attendant. Get me a couple of writers."

Indeed, writing is not often easy or fun, and those of us in business are usually too busy to give it the time that it *seems* to demand. Even people like me who list "writer" as a profession on our 1040 Form often wish *we* had staff writers on call to handle those difficult letters, memos, and e-mails that seem to pile up.

However, most of us—even in large organizations—have to do what this introduction has already said: Be our own communication department. We have to take personal responsibility for the stream of writing tasks that crosses our physical and virtual desktops.

That's probably as it should be. As designer, "information architect," and entrepreneur Richard Saul Wurman said, "You shortchange yourself if you think that writing is 'someone else's problem.' . . . Even if your job description says nothing about writing, by regarding yourself as a writer, even privately, you can take advantage of the discipline of the craft."

This quotation is wonderful for two words in particular and for its overall message:

- One key word is *discipline*. Writing *is* a discipline—in the sense that chemistry is a discipline or yoga is a discipline—and like them, it *requires* discipline. As Larry Gelbart, creator of the "M*A*S*H" TV series, has said, "How to begin a writing project? Put your ass down in your chair, and hope that your head gets the message." Fortunately, the rest of this introduction will show you how to make that discipline a lot less painful.
- The other key word in Wurman's quotation is *craft*. A craft is something that lies somewhere between an art and a science. A good potter, for example, needs both an eye for beauty and a knowledge of the chemistry and physics of clay. Similarly, a good writer needs

both an "ear" for the language (the competence discussed earlier) and a knowledge of what makes an effective and efficient writing process.

- Wurman's overall message is important because as a teacher and trainer, I've seen over and over again that people become what they call themselves. A young person who thinks of himself as a failure may well fulfill that prophecy. A young person who thinks of herself as a success may well succeed. One university writing teacher I know has her students sign their essays not in the usual place at the top but at the bottom, followed by a comma and the word *Writer*. She believes, as Wurman and I do, that "regarding yourself as a writer, even privately" lets you "take advantage of the discipline of the craft."

As this introduction has already suggested, what probably keeps most of us from regarding ourselves as writers is the belief that the ability to write well is a talent or a gift. For some, it surely is: The great novelist, poet, or playwright is doubtless born as much as made. But the everyday business writing that you and I do—the writing that gets the world's work done—requires no special gift. As researcher Frank Smith wrote, "It is a mistake to regard the thinking that underlies writing as something special, as a unique kind of activity that calls for unusual efforts and abilities."

MANAGING YOUR WRITING TIME

Managing writing is largely a matter of managing time. Writing is a process, occurring over time, and like any process, it can be done efficiently or inefficiently. Unfortunately, most of us have a pretty inefficient writing process.

That's because we try to get each word, each sentence, right the first time. Given a letter to write, we begin with the first sentence. *"What do I want to say? I'll try a word or two. Is this sentence going to work? Maybe not. Better backspace and start again. Another word, then another. Better.*

Figure I-1   One-stage writing.

A third word. Spelled correctly? Better check. OK, go on. A verb. Agree with subject? What next?" And so it goes, word by word, sentence by sentence, through the letter. In an hour of writing, as shown in Figure I-1, we might spend five minutes this way on each of a dozen sentences.

An Eastern Washington University research survey reported that "ineffective writers revise and plan almost entirely in the context of the individual sentence." "For the ineffective writer," the report continued, "drafting proceeds as a linear production of single sentences that typically adds up to a first-and-final draft."

That's like building a house by starting with the front door—planning, building, finishing the door, even washing the little window in it—before even breaking ground for the rest of the building. No wonder most of us have so much trouble writing.

Efficient, effective writers take better charge of their writing time; they *manage* their writing. Like homebuilders, they spend time planning before they start construction, and once they're into construction, they don't try to do all the finishing touches—such as washing the windows—as they go.

Many good writers break their writing process into three main stages—*planning, drafting,* and *revising*—with more time spent at the first and third stages than at the second. My friend Lee Clark Johns, in her excellent book *The Writing Coach*, reported a study of one professional writer who spent his writing time this way:

- 40 percent "prewriting" (planning)
- 20 percent "writing" (drafting)
- 40 percent "rewriting" (revising)

Many good writers also build in some *management* time at the beginning and the end of the process, and some *break* time in the middle.

OK, now we have a plan. So let's put a timeline on it. *Personnel Journal* has reported that the average business letter or memo takes 54 minutes to write, so let's round that up to an hour. As shown in Figure I-2, let's (somewhat arbitrarily) assign time this way:

- 20 minutes of that hour to *planning*
- 5 minutes to *drafting*
- 25 minutes to *revising*

Let's build in a five-minute *break* between drafting and revising and call the remaining five minutes *managing,* splitting it between the beginning and end of the hour. Rather than spending five minutes on each of a

Figure I-2   Five-stage writing.

dozen sentences, we'll spend each five minutes doing some very specific managing, planning, drafting, "breaking," or revising work.

And that will be the basis for this course. As we move through the 12 chapters of this book, we'll be moving through the 12 five-minute segments of a typical writing hour. For each segment, you'll learn some very specific, very practical, "warm worms" tools to use at that point in your writing process. By the end of this 36-hour course, you'll have an efficient, effective method for doing on-the-job writing, and you'll have a toolbox of powerful tools to use along the way.

THE LAW OF THE NEXT ACTION

There's one more powerful advantage of five-stage writing—especially when it's further divided into the 12 steps that are the basis for this book. As Fergus O'Connell wrote in his strategy book, *The Competitive Advantage of Common Sense*, "To do anything requires a sequence of events. Knowing this gives you the skills to plan, prioritize, accelerate projects, and get many things done at the same time."

I call this the *law of the next action*. This concept comes from David Allen's book *Getting Things Done: The Art of Stress-Free Productivity*, one of my top-five most useful business resources. The heart of Allen's work-management method is determining, for each of your projects, the next physical action.

As Allen pointed out, you can't really "do" a project, such as buy a new Blu-ray player, for example. What you *can* do is determine the next action, such as look up Ruth Ann's number so that you can call her and ask where she got the great deal she was talking about. Many projects in our lives look overly daunting, get repeatedly postponed, and cause us a lot of anxiety in the process because we haven't thought about, and written down, what the next physical action is. For example, using Allen's method, I currently have a list of 19 active projects—low for me because I've put so many projects on inactive status so that I could focus on the single project of writing this book—and I've listed the next physical action required for each of them.

Figure I-3   Susan's days are built upon a series of short-term goals.

Those active projects no longer haunt me any more than my inactive ones do for two reasons:

- They're written down outside my head.
- Whenever I want a break from writing this book, I can move forward on any of the other 18 projects simply by taking the next physical action.

I don't carry the law of the next action as far as Susan does in Figure I-3 (and David Allen has assured me that he doesn't either). Like Susan, however, I've learned the value of building workdays around a series of short-term goals that eventually add up to long-term results.

That's what the five-stage, 12-step writing process model does: it takes what is often the scary job of writing a document and breaks it into a series of next actions. You don't have to think of yourself sitting down and spending an hour writing a letter. You just have to spend a couple of minutes on the first "next action": *managing* the time you'll take to do the letter. After you've done that, you can go do something else if you want or need to—because you know that all you have to do next on the letter is the first five-minute task in the planning stage. And so on.

On her blog Writing English, Judy Rose wrote, "I like to break the task [of writing] into smaller steps—'*doable doses*,' as James Taylor calls them in one of his early songs. If writing doesn't come easily to you, then thinking about the whole thing is too daunting. One little step is '*doable*.'"

And author John Gregory Dunne wrote that "writing is manual labor of the mind: a job, like laying pipe." Exactly. Nobody can lay a pipeline. All they can do is lay the next length of pipe. Even eating an elephant is easier if you do it one spoonful at a time.

THE 12 STEPS

Enough background. Now that you know why we're going to divide the writing process into 12 steps, you need to know what they are.

At the *managing* stage (perhaps 2 or 3 minutes for a one-hour writing job), remind yourself that you're a writer, that writing can be managed, and that it's largely a matter of managing time. Therefore, start with 12 on the clock, as shown in Figure I-4. Plan your next hour—remembering that if you choose, you can spread it over several hours, days, or even weeks.

At the *planning* stage (perhaps 20 minutes for a one-hour writing job):

Figure I-4   Manage your writing.

1. *Find the "we."* Define the community to which you and your reader belong. Decide how you and your reader are alike and different in personality, attitude, circumstances, and knowledge. Chapter 1 will give you tools for making these decisions.
2. *Make holes, not drills*—as a consultant once told a major tool manufacturer. That is, focus on the outcome you want, not the means you'll use to achieve it. Define your purpose. Chapter 2 will show you how.
3. *Get your stuff together.* Collect the information you'll use in your writing. You'll get some help in Chapter 3.
4. *Get your ducks in a row.* Organize your information so that you can give it to your reader in the most useful order. Chapter 4 will give you some good organizational strategies.

At the *drafting* stage (perhaps 5 minutes for a one-hour job):

5. *Do it wrong the first time.* Do a "quick and dirty draft" without editing. You'll learn why and how in Chapter 5.

At the *break* stage (perhaps another 5 minutes):

6. *Take a break and change hats.* Get away from your draft, even if for only a few minutes, and come back with a fresh perspective— your reader's perspective. Chapter 6 will provide some tips for making the most of the break.

At the *revising* stage (perhaps 25 minutes):

7. *Signal your turns.* Just as if you were driving the lead vehicle in a convoy, you're leading your reader through new territory. Use "turn signals" to guide your reader from sentence to sentence. Chapter 7 will teach you this especially powerful tool.
8. *Say what you mean.* Put the point of your sentences in the subjects and verbs. Don't worry: Chapter 8 will remind you how to recognize subjects and verbs and show you how their effective use can strengthen your message.

9. *Pay by the word.* Make your sentences economical. You'll learn the tools for doing so in Chapter 9.
10. *Translate into English.* Keep your words simple. (Lee Iacocca put steps 9 and 10 in one "commandment of good management": "Say it in English and keep it short.") Chapter 10 will be your translation guide.
11. *Finish the job.* Check your spelling, punctuation, and mechanics. You'll get a quick refresher course in Chapter 11.

Finally, at the *managing* stage again (2 to 3 minutes):

12. *Manage your writing.* Evaluate the process you've just finished. Figure out how to improve it next time. You'll get help from Chapter 12.

Notice that these 12 steps take the same amount of time as the "one-stage" sentence-by-sentence method that many ordinary writers use. In fact, most people who have learned this method tell me that by managing their writing process, they're able to write faster. But even if you don't write faster, you'll be able to write more efficiently and effectively. You'll be able to use your writing to make good things happen for you and your organization. As writer Margaret Atwood said, "A word after a word after a word is power."

MANAGE YOUR WRITING

That's all there is to it. If you quit the course at this point (I hope you don't), you'll have already received maybe half its value. You've already learned three important lessons:

1. Writing is a process you can manage.
2. You should tackle writing jobs not all at once but in stages.
3. You should spend more time in the planning and revising stages than in the drafting stage.

The rest of this book consists of learning specific tools to use at these stages.

You also know already what to do in the first two or three minutes of a typical writing hour:

- Remind yourself that you're a writer and that writing can be managed.
- Allocate time for the 12 steps of the writing process.

Completing this important step will make you not only a better manager of your writing but also a better manager of everything else: people, projects, money, time. In their book *What They Really Teach You at the Harvard Business School* Francis J. Kelly and Heather Mayfield Kelly pointed out that "too often, we make major communications decisions without thinking them through at all. Or we just say or write whatever first comes to mind. . . . There are always choices to be made. The most effective managers will make them quickly, but also wisely."

MANAGE YOUR WRITING *TODAY*

Start with the very next writing job you have to do. Instead of diving right in and working on the first sentence, stop for a couple minutes and do some writing management: remind yourself that you're a writer, that writing can be managed, and that it's largely a matter of managing time. Then set up blocks of time for planning, drafting, and revising—with more time allocated for planning and revising than for drafting. Give yourself at least one break, between the drafting and revising stages.

When you've finished the writing job, take a few minutes to evaluate how the process worked for you. Don't worry if writing this way seemed awkward or unproductive at first; we all have a lot of old habits to replace. With practice and time, you'll become a much more effective and efficient writer.

1

FIND THE "WE"

Manage Your Relationship with Your Reader

Speaker Joe Griffith once told a story about the FBI under J. Edgar Hoover: "A young FBI man was put in charge of the FBI's supply department. In an effort to cut cost, he reduced the size of memo paper.

"One of the new memo sheets ended up on J. Edgar Hoover's desk. He disliked it immediately and wrote on the narrow margin, 'Watch the borders.'

"His message was misinterpreted. For the next six weeks, it was extremely difficult to enter the United States by road from either Mexico or Canada."

Such misunderstandings happen all the time in organizations large and small. Most result from poor planning. You'll recall that in the Introduction I divided the writing process into five stages: managing, planning, drafting, breaking, and revising—and then back to managing again. This chapter begins the planning stage, a stage that should take perhaps 20 minutes of a typical writing hour.

You may be a one-stage writer, used to starting your writing process by immediately drafting and revising the first sentence of your document.

If so, you may be afraid or suspicious of postponing drafting for as long as 20 minutes. You may be saying, "I can't afford to spend a third of my writing time without actually *writing* the thing." As communication consultant Lee Clark Johns has commented, "People often say, 'I don't have time to plan.' But if you want to become a reader-friendly writer, you don't have time *not* to plan."

I agree absolutely. Remember the old business saying: "To fail to plan is to plan to fail."

As shown in Figure 1-1, you begin the planning stage with the five-minute step I call "Find the 'We.'" This step is about defining the main relationship in writing: the relationship between writer(s) and reader(s). This relationship needs to be defined before any other meaningful decisions can be made. Jay Sidhu, CEO of Sovereign Bank, said it this way: "Communication is in the mind of the recipient: you're just making noise if the other person doesn't hear you."

Several decades ago, when the United States and the USSR were planning their first joint space mission, planners thought hard about how the language barrier would be crossed, especially in the kinds of perilous situations that could occur in early space flight. Naturally, the American

Figure 1-1   Find the "we."

astronauts were taught Russian, and the Soviet cosmonauts were taught English. But which language should be used when and by whom?

The answer may surprise you. After extensive study, NASA announced that the U.S. crew would always speak Russian, and the Soviet crew would always speak English. Why? Because the speaker, who knew what he wanted to say, could most easily do the work of mental translation. With lives at stake, the listener should not have to *both* mentally translate *and* absorb new information.

This principle applies to everything we write, even to speakers of our own language. We know what we want to say, so we bear the burden of making our message as easy as possible for our reader to understand.

On his Entrepreneur's Journey blog, Jon Symons wrote, "By far the most important skill of a writer is the ability to get inside the head of her reader. It is to be able to march in lockstep with the experience of your readers as they make their way through your copy. You are writing for them after all. You can write solely to express yourself, but if you want to make money in your business you will need to write for an audience."

A helpful term that has entered the business vocabulary in the last decade or two is *internal customer*. This term is helpful because it reminds us that we have to treat every reader as a *customer*. In fact, Tom Peters has argued that everyone in business, even an employee of a large company, should think of herself as a professional service firm, with clients or customers. And while the customer may not always be right, it's important to treat customers as if they are. We need to make it as easy and as stress-free as possible for the customer to do business with us. My friend Oliver E. Nelson Jr., account executive at Energy Systems Group, taught me what I've begun to think of as "Nelson's golden rule": "Write unto others as you would have them write unto you."

To follow this rule, we first need to understand *our* customer—our reader. As Lee Woods said on his blog Web Content That Sells, "The realtor's catchphrase has always been 'location, location, location.' For us, as writers writing to persuade a world of people to sign up, the catchphrase is 'audience, audience, audience.'"

Figure 1-2   The sender-receiver model.

COMMUNICATION AND COMMUNITY

Most of us in business have heard the advice to make our communication not *I*-centered but *you*-centered. Most business writing textbooks, including ones that I've written, tell us to focus not on the sender but on the receiver. They tell us to write not "I will send you a check" but "You will receive a check."

This advice is good. But it's not good enough. It's based on an incomplete model of the communication process, a model that can be diagrammed as in Figure 1-2.

But this model and the advice based on it ignore the fact that we in business are never isolated writers or speakers communicating with isolated readers or listeners. We communicate within organizations—ideally within *communities.* The relationship between sender and receiver always has to be thought of in a larger context, as shown in Figure 1-3.

Figure 1-3   The community model.

As Peter Drucker said in his classic book *Management*, "There can be no communication if it is conceived as going from the 'I' to the 'Thou.' Communication works only from one member of 'us' to another."

It's no accident that the words *communication* and *community* both come from the same Indo-European roots: *ko* and *mei* (pronounced "may"), meaning "together" and "change." (My company, Komei, Inc., is named after this fact.) A community is a group of people who "change together." Communication is what allows communities to change and what keeps them together *as* they change.

Native American cultures traditionally have known that community is necessary for communication to happen. Thomas W. Cooper wrote that for Native peoples, "Without genuine communion [another "*ko-mei*" word], there could be no meaningful communication. Thus the entire communication ethic was firmly based on spiritual communion."

But communication is not only necessary to community, it also *creates* community. If the quotation in the preceding paragraph was uncomfortably mystical for you, consider this one by dollars-and-cents reengineering guru James Champy: "It is authentic communication that brings people together into a community—listening, responding, confronting, asserting, and disputing—engaged in the perpetual process of change."

So the best business communication is not just *I*-centered or *you*-centered—it is *we*-centered. To make our e-mails, letters, and reports more *we*-centered, we need to ask two questions.

The first is, "To what community do my reader(s) and I both belong?" Are we members of the same team? Are we shareholders of the same company? Are we members of the same profession? In short, what makes us *us*? Try to find the smallest, most specific community that answers this question.

This is a practical, "warm worms" question. You'll find that if you define community at the very beginning of the writing process, all kinds of other decisions will fall into place for you. Difficult pieces of writing suddenly will become easier if instead of focusing on the antagonisms or differences between you and your reader(s), you focus on the community you're both part of, on the similarities you share. Even if you're angry at your reader and have a complaint about your reader's performance, you'll find that you can frame your message in the context of what you both want to happen—larger market share, say, or better work environment.

Lee Wood, former writer for Resort Condominiums International, said, "Writing is always an extension of the relationship you have with a person." She noted that such a focus is especially important now, with so many organizations experiencing great change.

Some writers find it helpful at this step in the process to draw a circle on a piece of scratch paper. Label it with the name of the community you share with your audience. Then around that circle draw circles for any larger communities of secondary audience members. Will a memo for your team, for example, also be read by higher management outside the team? (Remember that often you have a secondary audience that will exist only in the future, when someone takes advantage of the relative permanence of writing to check what you are writing in the present.)

Add to the diagram an arrow to represent your communication. Are you bringing information into the community from outside? Are you taking information the other direction, from inside out? Are you moving information from point to point *within* the community? You can use your sketch as a visual aid throughout the rest of your writing process.

The second important question to ask at this step is, "Within this community, how are my reader(s) alike and different?" Specifically, consider how you and your reader(s) are alike and different in four ways: personality, attitude, circumstances, and knowledge. To remember them, think of the acronym *PACK* as you "pack" for your journey around the clock face through the rest of the writing process.

PERSONALITY

The first dimension in which to consider similarities and differences is personality. The most used way of categorizing personality is the Myers-

Briggs Type Indicator (MBTI), employed in many organizations. The MBTI measures personality on four scales:

- **Extroversion (E) or introversion (I):** Roughly whether one draws energy from other people (E) or from within oneself (I).
- **Sensing (S) or intuition (N):** Roughly whether one draws information from the senses (S) or from intuition (N).
- **Thinking (T) or feeling (F):** Roughly whether one makes decisions based on logic (T) or on emotions (F).
- **Judgment (J) or perception (P):** Roughly whether one sets priorities rationally (J) or spontaneously (P).

Together, these four pairs of personality traits produce 16 combinations, or *types*. Although certain professions tend to attract certain types, this tendency is by no means absolute. A professional colleague of mine, an Air Force major who worked at the War College, once told me that among generals and admirals in the U.S. armed forces, all 16 MBTI types were represented.

If you know your MBTI type and those of your readers, you're especially fortunate: you'll be able to answer the "personality" question with great precision. If you know only your own type and can make a decent guess about those of your readers, you'll still be able to do excellent planning. Even if you've never heard of the MBTI, however, your general people skills will allow you to make very good decisions at this step—and you'll be able to understand much of the following advice, based on the research of communication consultant Dan Dieterich:

- If you're an *extrovert*, you may need to get all your thoughts on paper very early; you may, in fact, "think by writing." Thus you may want to write a very rough draft as part of step 3 and then reorganize it in step 4 so that you'll be able to write a much more organized draft in step 5. When you write to introverts, be sure to build community. Be careful not to overwhelm them with your position.

- If you're an *introvert*, you may find it hard to move out of the planning stage into "quick and dirty" drafting. You'll be helped by the advice, in step 5, about drafting without editing. When you write to extroverts, try to overcome your reticence by projecting self-assurance.
- If you're a *sensor*, be sure to move beyond the specific details in your writing to generalizations or conclusions. Be careful about trying to apply writing "rules" too rigidly; realize that you need to adapt to your specific writing situation. Make sure that you postpone your concern with spelling, punctuation, and mechanics until step 11, where it belongs. When you write to intuitives, focus on your main point or points, not on details.
- If you're an *intuitive*, make sure, at step 3, to gather a thorough list of facts and specific details. When writing to sensors, make sure to include enough details to support your main point or points.
- If you're a *thinker*, be sure to pay attention to the next section of this chapter, "Attitude." When writing to feelers, show empathy.
- If you're a *feeler*, you may need to be more structured and less sentimental. Pay special attention to step 4 of the writing process. When writing to thinkers, make your message clear and logical.
- If you're a *judger*, you may rush into the drafting stage without enough careful planning. When you revise your drafts, make sure that you thoroughly "change hats" from writer to reader in step 6. When writing to perceivers, be sure to be flexible. (Incidentally, as a judger, you'll naturally embrace the five-stage, 12-step method outlined in this book, but you'll need to keep reminding yourself that every situation is different and that flexibility is important.)
- If you're a *perceiver*, you may need to focus on your purpose and be concise. Give special attention to step 2 in the planning stage and step 9 in the revising stage. When writing to judging types, don't be afraid to come to a conclusion and express it forceably. (Incidentally, as a perceiver, you may find this book's five-stage, 12-step method rigid and difficult, but practicing it, at least for a while, will give your writing process some needed structure. Then you should feel free to modify it to suit your own personality.)

ATTITUDE

Some years ago, I was listening to one of my favorite radio programs while I worked on another business writing book. The program host, a skilled writer, spoke a short sentence about writing that was absolutely perfect for the chapter I was writing, so I immediately jotted it down.

The sentence was short enough that I knew I could legally and ethically quote it in my book—giving the host credit, of course—without getting his permission. But because I had only heard, not read, the sentence, I wanted to give the host a chance to see what I had written and to correct or revise the sentence if he wished. So I wrote him a letter. And because I was a real fan of his show, I turned it into a fan letter as well as an informational letter. After giving him the chance to review the quotation, I spent the rest of about two pages talking about the things I especially liked about the show and comparing it to some programs I had listened to as a child.

In a couple of weeks, I got back a two-sentence letter, not from the host but from a member of his production staff:

_____ Public Radio
Dear Mr. Davis:
We are flattered that you wish to include part of _____'s monologue in the textbook that you are writing, but it is Mr. _____'s policy not to give out the text of his _____ monologues. The main purpose behind our show is entertainment, as you well know, and we do not feel that it would make appropriate teaching materials.
Yours truly,

_____

I was ticked off—but not because the host wouldn't confirm the quotation. I knew I could legally and ethically use the sentence anyway. I was annoyed that the writer of the letter was condescendingly telling me how to do my job. Who was this person to tell me what would make "appropriate teaching materials"? I'm a textbook writer; she's a radio producer. I hadn't told her how to do *her* job!

And I also was annoyed that the "fan letter" content of my letter hadn't even been acknowledged.

Now don't get me wrong. I don't think at all that the writer of the letter meant to insult me. I suspect, instead, that she was a one-stage writer with a pile of mail to answer. She didn't take the time to consider her relationship with me—and as always, not to decide is to decide. If she'd thought about it, she'd have realized that my public radio station would twice a year be asking me for money—in part to support her show. If she'd thought about our attitudes, hers and mine (hers: rushed; mine: supportive and eager), she wouldn't have unnecessarily alienated me. She would have left out the judgmental language about textbooks and the snippiness of "as you well know." And she would have added a brief response to my radio reminiscences and an acknowledgment that while she couldn't confirm the quotation, she realized that I was free to use it anyway.

You see, all of us come to everything we write and read as people, with feelings and attitudes. Too often, as business writers, we forget that, thinking of ourselves and our readers not as people but as profit centers or as boxes on a line-and-block chart.

Instead, as you begin a writing job, ask what feelings about this communication you and your audience share. What feelings *don't* you share? Some writing and speaking is like paddling downstream with the current of your audience's attitudes; some is like paddling upstream against the current. Businessman Donald Walton wrote, "Keep in mind at all times that nobody (except you) cares a hoot about what *you* want. The people you're writing to care only about what will be good for them. You have to figure out carefully what that is, and then tell them about it. If you do that consistently, they'll like you. Also, they'll think you're smart. Because you are."

One good tool to use in assessing your readers' attitudes is to ask what need your writing will be filling for them. As you may know, according to psychologist Abraham Maslow, all human beings have the same basic needs that they strive to satisfy. These needs are arranged, says Maslow, in a hierarchy, as shown in Figure 1-4. The needs at the bot-

Figure 1-4   Maslow's hierarchy of needs.

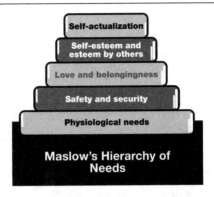

tom of Maslow's "pyramid" come first, but as they are satisfied, "higher" needs emerge.

Ask yourself which of these needs your piece of writing will satisfy for your audience. By way of illustration, consider the story that entrepreneur Peter Hay told about men's clothing tycoon Max Hart. According to Hay, Hart "summoned his advertising manager to complain about his latest campaign: 'Nobody reads that much copy,' he asserted.

"The ad manager begged to differ. 'I'll bet you ten dollars, Mr. Hart, that I can write a whole newspaper page of solid type, and you will read every word of it.' Hart eagerly accepted the bet.

"'I won't have to write even a paragraph to prove my point,' the ad man continued. 'I'll just give you the heading:

"This Page Is All About Max Hart.'"

The advertising manager had clearly diagnosed that his boss (like other people whose lower-level needs have been met) had a need for self-esteem and the esteem of others. The proposed heading was targeted directly at that need.

But whether or not you consciously use Maslow's hierarchy of needs, if you invest, at the planning stage, even a few seconds in considering your readers' attitudes, your writing is guaranteed to be more effective. As advertising legend David Ogilvy wrote, "The most effective leader is the one who satisfies the psychological needs of his followers."

CIRCUMSTANCES

Several times in my career I've heard a story—probably an "urban legend"—about the testing of a new fighter plane. According to the story, the U.S. Air Force had contracted for a new fighter. The manufacturer had produced several prototypes to flight-test before full production could begin.

Everything was going smoothly until suddenly a problem arose. A test pilot had radioed in that he was bailing out, but didn't, and was killed in the crash. Flight tests, of course, stopped until it could be discovered what was wrong with the ejection system.

On the ground, everything seemed to work correctly. But in the air, something had gone wrong. Finally, the Air Force and the manufacturer called in an outside consultant. The consultant arrived at the test site, climbed into the cockpit of one of the planes, and had the canopy lowered over him.

He noticed that on the canopy, just to his left, were the instructions for ejection: three easy steps. "Step 1: Pull the red lever below to release the canopy."

You may already see the problem. On the ground, you pull the red lever, and the canopy unlocks but just sits there. In the air, you pull the red lever, and—Whoosh!—the canopy is a mile behind you, along with instruction steps 2 and 3.

Fortunately, most of us aren't in the business of giving life-and-death instructions. But even in seemingly routine messages, we need to consider the circumstances in which the reader will be receiving our communication. If the communication is face-to-face, the circumstances are obvious: the room, the lighting, the acoustics, the time of day. However, the circumstances in which a *written* communication is received are just as important. For example, consider the following memo from one of my clients, a Fortune 100 company. I've changed only department names and numbers.

In order to have effective controls on automobile repairs and to insure proper and prompt payment of invoices, all repairs and purchase of tires for automobiles will be administered by Motor Pool, Department 680, effective March 1. Prior to taking your automobile to a vendor for work, contact Motor Pool, extension 6729, to obtain a purchase order and release. Complete a blanket purchase order release form with Department 680 as department ordering and price is to be marked advise, complete account code and department charge, then obtain buyer's signature.

Upon completion of form give a copy to the vendor when you take the vehicle in for the service. After the work has been completed check the bill to insure there are no arithmetic or extension discrepancies and verify that sales tax has not been included. On the bill state that service has been received, then have two signatures on the bill with the purchase order and release order number. When the invoice is correct and approved, send it to Motor Pool for processing.

If you have any questions, please contact me. Thanks for your assistance in this matter.

This memo went out to perhaps a thousand employees of a single plant. My client showed it to me six months later because it simply hadn't worked. Most employees simply weren't following the directions.

You don't need me to tell you what was wrong. The memo is wordy, hiding crucial steps in the middle of long paragraphs instead of displaying them openly in a numbered list, and a lot of sentence-level revisions are needed.

The biggest problem, however, is in the planning stage—specifically in the writer's failure to consider the circumstances in which employees would be reading the memo. I asked a company representative, "On the day the memo was received, how many employees needed repairs or tires for a company car and so could use the information that very day?" The answer was very few, maybe just two or three. For the remaining 997 or so, the memo had no immediate usefulness, so it was trashed or buried in a file cabinet. Three or six months later, when one of those 997 employees needed tires or car repairs, he or she might well have forgotten even receiving the memo, much less what it said.

My advice to the company was to consider the circumstances the readers would be in and not send a memo at all. Instead, I recommended that the company revise the purchase order form to make it self-instructional, put a pad of these forms in the glove compartment of each company car, and put a small sticker on the dashboard that said, "Need repairs or tires? Use the form in the glove compartment."

I can't claim a win on this one. The company didn't follow my advice. But I hope that the people I talked with became more aware that writing is never read in the *abstract*. It's always read in very specific *circumstances*.

Marketers, perhaps more than any other businesspeople, truly understand the importance of considering audience circumstances. According to David Graulich, on the public radio show *Marketplace*, a small disk-drive manufacturer, during a gigantic Las Vegas computer trade show, "arranged to have Las Vegas cab drivers ask their passengers, 'Do you know who makes the fastest disk drives?' If an employee of the manufacturer was in the cab when the driver asked the question, the cabbie got paid one hundred dollars. The company says it got a terrific response, with lots of people calling up to ask about the product, or to argue about whether their disk drive really was the fastest." The point? The manufacturer's marketers realized that at the trade show, a cab ride offered a rare "captive" situation, a distraction-free circumstance in which to get a marketing message through.

So at step 1, in your planning stage, spend at least a few seconds thinking about the circumstances in which your message will be read. Imagine your reader not just as a face (like the passport-style photos in some contact management programs) but as a complete person at a particular place and time. Ask yourself whether your message will be the only piece of business writing your reader receives this week or one of a hundred e-mails competing for her attention tomorrow morning. As writers Herbert E. Meyer and Jill M. Meyer put it, "A piece of writing gets one shot."

So picture your reader as he receives and reads your message. If you're lucky (or unlucky) enough to have a reader like the one shown in Figure 1-5, that's how to imagine him.

Follow the advice of famed sports agent Mark H. McCormack: "Most people are so engrossed in the message they are trying to convey

Figure 1-5   Whether one enjoys reading reports has a lot to do with *how* one reads them.

that they forget to step out of themselves and think about the reader. The most effective communicators try to visualize the person reading and reacting to their writing."

So give it a try. The more you can imagine the reader's circumstances, the richer, clearer picture you'll have of your reader and the more effective your writing will be.

KNOWLEDGE

The fourth and last dimension in which to consider how you are like and unlike your reader(s) is knowledge. Whenever you write something to a reader, the two of you have to have some knowledge in common, or communication isn't possible. To be part of the necessary community, you have to share some knowledge.

However, there also has to be some knowledge you *don't* have in common. If you and your reader already share total knowledge of the subject, communication isn't necessary. As I've gotten older, I've learned why older married couples don't always talk a lot with each other. It's not necessarily because they are bored with each other or because they've run out of things to say. It's because in many situations each of them already knows what the other is thinking. Normally in business, though, you don't have that level of intimacy. There's a knowledge gap somewhere—and it's that gap that much business writing is designed to bridge.

Some years ago a manager at one of my client companies showed me a feedback form the company had received about one of its software manuals. In the manual, the writer had defined the term *default value.*

As you may know, a default value is a preset variable. In Microsoft Word, for example, the default value for the left margin is 1.25 inches. If you want a 1.0-inch or 1.5- or 2.0-inch margin instead, you can easily change the setting to your desired width. But if you don't change it, you get the default width of 1.25 inches.

The writer of the manual had been more creative than that. The manual defined *default value* by analogy. It said, suppose that you stop at the same coffee shop on your way to work every morning, and you almost always order a doughnut and a cup of coffee. Soon that becomes your "usual"— your default value for breakfast. Even if you just grunt, they'll bring you a doughnut and coffee. If on some days you ask for a muffin instead, you'll get it. But unless you do that often, a doughnut remains the default value.

That manual, with its explanation of default values, found its way to Japan. A Japanese employee of the company filled out the feedback form at the end of the manual and returned it to company headquarters in the United States. He wrote the following inquiry:

> Sorry inconvenience your time. Concerning explanation of you in page 95 "Default values" I have difficulty explaining to my customer what is a doughnut and what is a muffin. Can you send me both each? How is it shown in listing?
> Thankfully,

And then a signature, in Japanese characters. Now, I'm confident that the feedback form was written for humorous effect, a way of pulling the corporate leg. I think the use of "Japanese English" was a part of the joke. But whether the feedback was serious or not, it makes an important point. If you're trying to explain default values by comparing them to doughnuts and muffins, you'd better make sure that your audience knows what doughnuts and muffins are. If not, you've made your message *less* clear.

We all have our own "doughnuts" and "muffins." Whether our audience is across the world or across the hall, we all have words and concepts whose meanings are obvious to us but will not necessarily be obvious to our audience. Some technical writers and editors use an acronym, *COIK*, that stands for "Clear Only If Known." You'll sometimes find that an editor has scribbled "COIK" beside a passage that will be perfectly clear to any reader who already shares the writer's knowledge (and thus doesn't need to read the passage in the first place) but not at all clear to a reader who *doesn't* share that knowledge.

If the COIK material consists of just a technical term here and there, it can be corrected in the revising stage. However, eliminating COIK material often involves substantial rewriting. It's more efficient to avoid COIK material in the first place by making consideration of your audience's knowledge an important part of step 1, "Find the 'We,'" in the planning stage.

If you write for audiences around the world—and more and more business writers now do—Appendix B, "Manage Your Global Writing," will give you a framework for more effective international business communication.

Exercise

The following questions will test your understanding of this chapter. The final examination for this course will include similar questions.

1. Why is defining your community—your relationship with your reader(s)—the first step in the planning stage?
   a. It comes first alphabetically.
   b. It is represented by the *P* in the acronym *PACK.*
   c. All other planning decisions depend on it.
   d. It is the most difficult step.

2. Which of the following statements is most true?
    a. Community is necessary for communication.
    b. Communication is necessary for community.
    c. Both *a* and *b* are true.
    d. Neither *a* nor *b* is true.
3. In defining the community to which you and your reader(s) both belong, which of the following should you focus on?
    a. The largest possible community
    b. The smallest possible community
    c. The corporate community
    d. The international community
4. In thinking about your audience, which the following questions should you ask?
    a. How are my audience and I alike?
    b. How are my audience and I different?
    c. Both *a* and *b*
    d. Neither *a* nor *b*
5. When you and your reader(s) have different personality types, which of the following best expresses what you should do?
    a. Simply be yourself, in the confidence that your reader(s) will be able to adjust.
    b. Consider both your personality type and those of your readers, and adjust as necessary to your readers' personalities.
    c. Ignore personality differences, because they are unimportant in business communication.
    d. Find common ground with your reader(s) in a third personality type.
6. If you're a *feeler* writing to a *thinker*, which of the following should you do?
    a. Avoid being overly sentimental.
    b. Make sure that you support your opinions logically.
    c. Make your thinking process clear.
    d. All of the above
7. Which of the following statements about attitudes is most true?
    a. Similarities and differences between your attitude and that of your audience should be considered at the planning stage.

     b. Consideration of similarities and differences between your attitude and that of your audience should be postponed until the revision stage.

     c. Consideration of attitudes should not enter into the business writing process.

     d. None of the above

8. **Which of the following statements about the Maslow hierarchy of needs is most true?**

     a. It is a handy checklist of punctuation rules.

     b. It can help you to assess how your writing can fill a need for your reader(s).

     c. It describes the five needed stages in the writing process.

     d. None of the above

9. **In visualizing your reader(s), which of the following statements is most true?**

     a. You should visualize your reader(s) at their best.

     b. You should visualize your reader(s) at their worst.

     c. You should visualize your reader(s) reading and reacting to your message.

     d. You should focus on your reader's face.

10. **Which of the following best expresses the meaning of the acronym *COIK*?**

     a. COIK material will be understandable by the reader(s) only if they already know it.

     b. COIK material is adjusted to the four elements of the personality of your reader(s).

     c. COIK material considers circumstances, opportunities, intelligence, and knowledge of your reader(s).

     d. None of the above

MANAGE YOUR WRITING *TODAY*

Now that you've checked your understanding of Chapter 1, you should put it into practice right away.

- On the very next writing job you have to do, begin with some writing management: Remind yourself that you're a writer, that writing can be managed, and that it's largely a matter of managing time. Set up blocks of time for planning, drafting, and revising—with more time allocated for planning and revising than for drafting.

- Then begin the planning stage by "finding the 'we.'" Take perhaps five minutes to ask yourself, "What is the smallest community to which my audience and I both belong?" and "How are my audience and I alike and different in the four PACK dimensions: personality, attitude, circumstances, and knowledge?" Answer these questions very explicitly this first time, making notes about your answers.
- Next go ahead and do the rest of your planning, thinking about purpose, content, and organization. (You'll learn some more specific planning methods in the next three chapters.)
- Then draft your document with as little editing as possible.
- Take a break.
- Then revise it.

When you've finished the writing job, take a few minutes to evaluate how the process worked for you. Evaluate especially whether "finding the 'we'" resulted in a more effective message at the end.

2

MAKE HOLES, NOT DRILLS

Manage with Purpose

Accprding to business legend, a large tool manufacturer once called in a consulting team to look at the company's whole operation, from drawing board to packing case. At the exit interview, the lead consultant addressed the tool company's executives. "Ladies and gentlemen," he said, "the most important thing you need to remember is that you're not in the business of making drills. You're in the business of making holes."

The consultant probably meant two things. First, he was stressing the importance of knowing what business you're really in. In nineteenth-century America, the railroad companies were wealthy and powerful beyond imagination. If you had asked one of the railroad barons what business he was in, he would have said "the railroad business." Wrong answer. He would have been thinking much too narrowly. If, instead, those powerful railroad companies had thought of themselves as being in the transportation business, they might have survived and ended up owning airlines, trucking firms, and overnight express companies. Similarly, the consultant was telling the tool manufacturer that it should define itself broadly. If a technology comes along to replace the drill (lasers, perhaps?), the company should be prepared to dump drill making and move on.

This is important advice. But more important to us as business writers is the second thing that consultant probably meant. He meant that it's crucial to know the *purpose* of what you're doing. If you focus on just making drills, it'll be too easy to forget why your customer wants to buy a drill in the first place. Some major tool manufacturers truly have learned this lesson: they give away thousands of free project plans in order to give their customers reasons to drill holes.

Most of us business writers haven't learned this lesson. If a coworker interrupts us while we're writing a letter and asks, "What are you doing?" most of us will answer, "Writing a letter." This response focuses on the piece of writing—the tool—itself, not on its purpose. The result: our writing often misses the chance to be as effective as it could be. At this crucial second step of the planning stage of the writing process, shown in Figure 2-1, don't ask yourself about the *document* you're going to write. Instead, ask yourself what effect you want to have on your reader(s). If a coworker interrupts your writing and asks what you're doing, be prepared to answer, "I'm trying to make this customer forgive us for the shipping mistake we made."

Figure 2-1   Make holes, not drills.

Make Holes,
Not Drills

For example, a common mistake in writing job application letters is failure to understand their purpose. Most job application letters should not be written for the purpose of getting a job but for the purpose of getting an interview. Getting the purpose right will help you to get on the interview list.

Thomas W. Cooper has written that Native American chief, actor, and activist Dan George "never wrote without a reason. . . . What was more important than George's words was that such words were born only of purpose. He had a purpose for silence, and a purpose for speaking." We should learn from this. We should learn not to speak or write until we have a clear sense why we're speaking or writing. Instead, we're too often like Jason in Figure 2-2, "Strong on 'how' and weak on 'why.'"

My friend Oliver E. Nelson Jr. of Energy Systems Group said, "Knowing what your purpose is not only makes the document better; it helps remove ego problems—because then you know what your job is, to get something done, not to make yourself look better."

Sports agent Mark McCormack wrote that "business memos usually have two purposes—either to project your ideas onto the company or to protect you from other people's ideas. Make your choice before you write

Figure 2-2   Jason is strong on "how" and weak on "why."

a word. Whether you're advancing your cause or defending your turf, your readers won't be clear about it unless you are." Although I don't find McCormack's two choices particularly helpful, I love his advice: Your readers won't be clear about your purpose unless you are.

That's our task for this five-minute segment of a typical writing hour. We need to be very clear about what we want. We've managed our writing process, and we've found the "we" by identifying the community that we share with our audience and the ways in which we and our audience are alike and different. Now it's time to focus on what we want—specifically on what we want our reader(s) to know or do as a result of reading our message. We need to remember Vincent McHugh's advice that "self-expression is for babies and seals, where it can be charming. A writer's business is to affect the reader."

In short, we need to focus on holes, not drills.

DEATH TO SUBJECT LINES

Some years ago a life insurance company got a new young CEO with a human resources background. Almost immediately he became concerned about the poor quality of memos coming across his desk. (This was, incidentally, in the very first year or two of e-mail, so most memos were still being written on paper.) The problem with these memos wasn't misspelling or incorrect punctuation or bad grammar; it was an overall lack of focus and clarity, making them difficult to get through. He asked me to work with him to turn the problem around. He wanted his company to be known as the best communicator in the business.

His first impulse, and mine, was to do massive training. But we remembered what psychologist Abraham Maslow (you'll remember him from Chapter 1) said: "If all you have is a hammer, everything looks like a nail." Therefore, instead of diving into training, we had a series of meetings with the CEO's team of senior vice presidents. Although we did end up doing some training, the most important thing we did was redesign the company's memo form.

The first problem with the old form was its heading: "Interoffice Correspondence." If you start to write on a form that begins with "Interoffice Correspondence," you get the subliminal message that you are supposed to do wordy, stuffy, pretentious writing (more about that in Chapter 10). So we gave our new form the simple heading "Memo."

The next things on the old form were "Date," "To," and "From." Fair enough. We left those alone. But the next line read "Subject," like 99 percent of the memos and 100 percent of the e-mail messages you've read. Subject lines began when file folders and file cabinets were introduced into business (before then, correspondence was done by hand and copied into large ledgers). Subject lines weren't invented for writers and readers but for file clerks. And they positively invite vagueness. As one of my trainees told me, "The hardest thing about writing memos is filling in the subject. So you just throw something in there. When the reader gets it, it's the part he or she reads first. And the subject line may not be what you want them to get out of it."

Therefore, we killed the subject line on the memo form.

But first we found a good replacement for it. Our memo form had a new line: "Purpose." To help the writer, we made the answer multiple-choice. Below "Purpose" we put two other lines, each with a check box before it:

Purpose:
❏ to tell you about _____ .
❏ to ask you to _____ .

The writer was to check either or both of these purposes and fill in the blank or blanks.

For the writer, the new form demanded that the "hole," not just the "drill," be considered right at the beginning of the writing process. If the writer of the memo about automobile tires and repairs in Chapter 1 had used this memo form, he might have checked both purposes and written the following:

Purpose:
- ☑ to tell you about the <u>new auto-repair policy.</u>
- ☑ to ask you to <u>do the following steps when you need repairs or tires.</u>

The obvious advantage of this purpose line was for the reader. When someone got a memo on the new form, she knew right up front whether she was just being told *about* something or being asked to *do* something. She could decide immediately whether to read the rest of the memo or set it aside for the moment or forever. When she did read the memo, she could read it with the purpose in mind.

Management consultant Bill Jensen wrote in his book *Simplicity,* "About 80 percent of your internal communication—meetings, teleconferences, presentations, emails, etc.—consists of

- Sharing information that does not require action, and/or
- Communicating something for which there is no discernible consequence if the recipient ignores it

"In other words, a lot of communication you thought was helpful may be seen as unfocused noise or just 'FYI' junk mail by your teammates." The new memo form allowed readers to screen out "noise" immediately. It allowed readers to ask immediately WIIFM?—What's in it for me?

However, the bigger advantage of the purpose line was for the writer. Having to think about your purpose at the beginning almost guarantees that your writing will be more effective. So whether or not you actually begin labeling your subject lines as purpose lines, do take five minutes or so at the beginning of planning any message to ask yourself, "What's my purpose: to tell my audience about something or to ask them to do something or both?"

Shortly after we designed the memo form, Mark McCormack's book *What They* Still *Don't Teach You in Harvard Business School* appeared with its list of the eight "toughest" messages to deliver: "(1) This is how you do it. (2) I want to sell you. (3) I goofed. (4) I have some bad news for you. (5) You did a great job. (6) Dear Boss, you're wrong. (7) This is my demand. (8) This is how you rate."

McCormack continued, "I would read a memo that began with any one of these sentences."

KO AND *MEI* COMMUNICATION

"It's not *what* she said; it's *how* she said it." "His *actions* are so loud, I can't hear what he's *saying*." "She *talked* a lot, but she didn't *say* anything."

Comments like these describe perhaps the most common kind of communication failure: the failure to balance the two main functions of communication. This failure can be largely avoided at this second step of the planning stage of the writing process. To communicate effectively, we need to find this balance.

As I said in Chapter 1, the word *communication* comes from the Indo-European roots *ko* and *mei* (pronounced "may"), meaning "together" and "change." Some communication takes place primarily for the *ko* function of building or maintaining relationships, of keeping a community together. For example, greetings exchanged with coworkers, such as "Hello" and "How are you?" have almost exclusively a *ko* function. (If you want to test whether "How are you?" has a *ko* function, try answering the question honestly and completely the next time someone asks it.)

Other communication takes place primarily for the *mei* function of changing something, of getting something done. For example, a faxed order for a pepperoni pizza (no anchovies) probably has exclusively a *mei* function.

Of course, most acts of communication have both functions. When we speak or write, we usually want both to maintain a relationship *and* to get something done. If you ask a coworker, "Tony, if you don't mind, would you please bring the first-quarter sales figures to the meeting?" you're trying to get the sales figures, but you're also trying to keep on good terms with Tony. Phrasing your request as a question and including the words "if you don't mind" and "please" reveal your *ko* purpose.

The use of such *ko* language by European-Americans interestingly led to a change in Native American communication. Thomas W. Cooper wrote, "It is somewhat ironic that the misrepresentative symbol of Native communication—a chief raising his open hand and saying 'How'—was in response to the white man's influence on the Native. The indigenous vocabulary did not include 'How.' But, since the settler and the soldier asked the Native so many questions—'How are you doing?' 'How is your family?' 'How are your crops?' 'How is your health?'—the Native sought to nullify this lengthy examination with one simple 'How?'"

Language experts have used a number of labels for what I call the *ko* and *mei* functions of communication: *social* and *practical, identity-focused* and *task-focused, relationship-oriented* and *content-oriented,* and *interactional* and *transactional.* Deborah Tannen, in such books as *You Just Don't Understand,* referred to these functions as the "meta-message" and the "message" and argued that women and men sometimes value them differently.

But to be effective in an organization, whether you're a woman or a man, you have to balance the *ko* and *mei* functions in what you say and write. To check your balance, ask yourself these questions:

1. Is my communication more relationship-oriented or more content-oriented? That is, do I tend to emphasize the *ko* function of togetherness or the *mei* function of change, of action, of getting things done?
2. If I'm chiefly a *ko* communicator, how can I become more confident, more assertive, and more willing to ask for a change in other people's actions or opinions?
3. If I'm chiefly a *mei* communicator, how can I become less abrupt, more supportive, more sensitive, and more willing to postpone immediate results for the sake of ongoing relationships?

THE LONG AND SHORT OF IT

American business is often criticized for its "short-termism." Fairly or unfairly, U.S. executives, boards of directors, and shareholders are charged with obsessive attention to the current quarter's numbers at the expense of longer-term growth. We're all victims of a "what have you done for me lately?" syndrome. Whether or not this is fair overall, it's certainly true of communication. In the talking and writing we do, most of us tend to focus on immediate short-term effects rather than long-term effects. We tend to speak or write for today or tomorrow, not for next year or next decade. To be more effective in business, we need to change this. We need to master long-term as well as short-term communication.

To understand the difference between long-term and short-term communication, let's consider how communication functions in living systems. All living systems, from single cells to the global ecosystem, share certain characteristics. Some of these characteristics have to do with how systems process information—how they communicate. In fact, communication is one of the things that make a system a system, not just a random collection of parts.

In her book *Leadership and the New Science*, Margaret J. Wheatley discussed this fact:

> For a system to remain alive, for the universe to move onward, information must be continually generated. If there is nothing new, or if the information that exists merely confirms what is, then the result will be death. Isolated systems wind down and decay, victims of the law of entropy. The fuel of life is new information—novelty— ordered into new structures. We need to have information coursing through our systems, disturbing the peace, imbuing everything it touches with new life.

Consider the living cell. In a cell, some information is long term, stored in the cell's DNA. As the cell reproduces, this information is communicated from generation to generation. The molecules that make up the cell may change, but this long-term information remains relatively constant. By contrast, some information in a cell is short term, in the form of electrical or chemical "messages" sent within the cell and between the cell and its environment. For example, such a message might carry information about temperature changes.

In an organization, too, some information is long term, relatively permanent, allowing the organization to preserve its identity even as its members come and go. James Moore, writing in *Fast Company* magazine, asked, "What is organizational DNA? It's the stuff, mostly intangible, that determines the basic character of a business. It's bred from the founders, saturates early employees, and often shapes behavior long after the pioneers have passed on."

By contrast, some information in an organization is short term, relatively temporary, allowing the organization to stay responsive and alive. To check your balance between long- and short-term communication, ask yourself these three questions:

1. Is my communication more short term or long term in its focus? That is, do I tend to communicate in order to build immediate relationships and get immediate results, or do I tend to ignore immediate goals in favor of a longer view?
2. If I'm a short-term communicator, how can I get a longer-term perspective? How can I start thinking more about long-term effects of my communication?
3. If I'm a long-term communicator, how can I focus more closely on the immediate relationships and short-term results that I need in order to realize my long-term goals and visions?

THE CORPORATE COMMUNICATION GRID

The two ways we've discussed of dividing communication—*ko* and *mei* and long term and short term—can be graphed in a matrix, or grid, as shown in Figure 2-3, resulting in four different kinds of communication.

The lower-left cell of the grid contains communication that is relatively short term and that has, as its main function, the *ko* function of creating or maintaining community. When you say "Hi" to a coworker, you're operating in this cell of the grid. I call this kind of communication *conversation*, although actual conversation usually has both *ko* and *mei* functions. In his book *The Postmodern Organization*, William Bergquist argued eloquently for the importance of conversation in an organization. "Goods and machines," he wrote, "are *parts* of the organization, whereas *conversations* are the essence of the organization."

Figure 2-3   Corporate communication grid.

This kind of "conversation" can be written as well as spoken. A letter to a supplier that begins "I certainly enjoyed talking with you yesterday; it was fascinating to hear about your trip to Kyrgyzstan," is a letter that begins with "conversation." In fact, for reasons mentioned in the Introduction to this book, more and more conversation is occurring in writing, especially in the form of e-mail.

Tom Peters devoted a full chapter of his book *Liberation Management* to CNN as a model of the new organization—Peters would say "disorganization"—required by these fast-changing times. His most striking snapshot is one taken in the early morning as several dozen executives and staffers in Atlanta and elsewhere conduct their daily scheduling meeting, refining a 30-page schedule document that has been drafted the night before. The atmosphere is casual, almost chaotic. Peters wrote that during the meeting he observed, most participants "were simultaneously reading newspapers. Side conversations were rife. The chatter was open, free and easy—consistent with the overriding emphasis on action."

Out of this apparent chaos, however, comes a document that literally redefines CNN with each new day. In this company without rigid hierarchies, the daily schedule establishes and reestablishes the shape of the organization. "It's only a minor exaggeration," wrote Peters, "to say that the document *is* the network."

Think about that. To say that an organization is created by communication—as noted in Chapter 1—is to say nothing new. Like any living system, an organization is held together by the information that flows back and forth among its components. But to say that an organization *is*, in fact, a *document*—a piece of business writing—is to say something *very* new. That's why I'm so committed to speaking, training, and writing about business writing. Business writing is more important today than ever. It's because writing literally *constitutes* the new organization.

The lower-right cell of the grid contains communication that is also relatively short term but that has as its main function the *mei* function of effecting change, of making something happen. Such communication is a kind of *correspondence*, although, of course, it includes not only many letters, memos, and e-mail messages but also much oral communication as well. Courses and books on business communication traditionally have emphasized this cell to the exclusion of the other three. In this book, I'm trying to remedy that problem.

The upper-left cell of the grid contains communication that is relatively long term and that exists primarily for *ko* purposes. I call this communication *covenant*. Covenant communication includes such documents as mission statements or values statements; it also includes the oral traditions of an organization—its myths and legends. All these forms of covenant communication have the effect of establishing and maintaining the long-term relationships among the members of the organization or between the organization and its various stakeholders. Jack Hawley, in his book *Reawakening the Spirit in Work*, wrote that "the leader's first task is to define reality, to make sense of the organization and its environment. As a leader . . . you're signer of a sacred covenant."

In recent years, one kind of covenant communication, the mission statement, has gotten a bad rap. *Dilbert* creator Scott Adams, for example, defined a mission statement as "a long awkward sentence that demonstrates management's inability to think clearly." "All good companies," said Adams, "have one." I myself was part of a group that helped an organization define a mission statement for itself, only to hear several months later about a fruitless two-hour search by two employees to find a copy of it. The lesson, of course, is that mission statements, like other forms of covenant communication, have to be *living* documents, continually communicated in many ways, spoken and written.

For example, in 1990, while producing an international video teleconference, I was referred to a person who was described to me as a "keeper of the corporate culture" at Apple. On a formal line-and-block chart, that person wouldn't have been especially prominent, but in the ongoing covenant communication of the company, he played a major role.

The upper-right cell of the grid contains communication that is also relatively long term but that exists primarily for the *mei* function of change. Such communication can be called *conception*. Conception communication includes vision statements, conceptions of what the organization ought to be changing *toward*.

You may be thinking, "What does this all have to do with me? I don't write mission, values, or vision statements every day." The point is that even when you think of yourself as engaged just in *correspondence*, you'll be more effective at it if you consider your organization's needs for *conversation*, *covenant*, and *conception* communication as well.

Exercise

The following questions will test your understanding of this chapter. The final examination for this course will include similar questions.

1. Why is defining your purpose the second step in the planning stage?
   a. It should be done after defining your community—writer and reader(s).
   b. It should be done before collecting and organizing the content of your message.
   c. Both *a* and *b* are true.
   d. Neither *a* nor *b* is true.
2. Why do subject lines in memos and e-mail messages cause problems?
   a. They weren't invented for the reader(s) of the message.
   b. They are often vague.

    c.   Both *a* and *b* are true.

    d.   Neither *a* nor *b* is true.

3. **Using the subject line to define the message's purpose benefits whom?**

    a.   The writer, because it encourages the writer to define her purpose

    b.   The reader, because it allows him to better screen and read the message

    c.   Both the writer and the reader

    d.   Neither the writer nor the reader

4. **Readers always want to know WIIFM. What do these letters stand for?**

    a.   Words, images, ideas, format, and mechanics

    b.   What's in it for me?

    c.   Whether included information facilitates metaphors

    d.   Neither *a*, *b*, nor *c*

5. **All communication has both *ko* and *mei* functions. What do these root words mean?**

    a.   Oral and written

    b.   Long term and short term

    c.   Communication and community

    d.   Together and change

6. **Most pieces of communication have what function?**

    a.   A community-building function

    b.   A change function

    c.   Both *a* and *b*

    d.   Neither *a* nor *b*

7. **Which of the following is probably *not* an example of "conversation" communication, as defined in this book?**

    a.   A birthday card

    b.   A discussion, over lunch, of your children's activities

    c.   A corporate mission statement

    d.   A question about the reader's family at the beginning of a business e-mail message

8. **Which of the following is probably *not* an example of "correspondence" communication, as defined in this book?**

    a.   A birthday card

    b.   A telephone call to order office supplies

    c. An e-mail message to order office supplies

    d. A faxed order for office supplies

9. Which of the following is probably *not* an example of "covenant" communication, as defined in this book?

    a. A mission statement

    b. An oral story of your company's founding

    c. A corporate privacy policy

    d. A profit-and-loss statement for the month

10. Which of the following is probably *not* an example of "conception" communication, as defined in this book?

    a. A speech by a CEO projecting five-year goals for the company

    b. A corporate vision statement

    c. A corporate history

    d. A written timeline of goals for the next 10 years

MANAGE YOUR WRITING *TODAY*

Now that you've checked your understanding of Chapter 2, you should put it into practice right away.

- On the very next writing job you have to do, begin with some writing management: Remind yourself that you are a writer, that writing can be managed, and that it is largely a matter of managing time. Set up blocks of time for planning, drafting, and revising—with more time allocated for planning and revising than for drafting.
- Then begin the planning stage by "finding the 'we.'" Take perhaps five minutes to ask yourself, "What is the smallest community to which my audience and I both belong?" and "How are my audience and I alike and different in the four PACK dimensions: personality, attitude, circumstances, and knowledge?"
- Then practice what you've learned in this chapter, taking perhaps five minutes to define the purpose of this piece of writing. Ask yourself, "Is my purpose to tell my reader(s) about something, ask my reader(s) to do something, or both? Will this piece of writing func-

tion as conversation, correspondence, covenant, or conception—or some combination of those?" Answer these questions very explicitly this first time, making notes about your answers.

- Next go ahead and do the rest of your planning, thinking about content and organization. (You'll learn some more specific planning methods in the next two chapters.)
- Then draft your document with as little editing as possible.
- Take a break.
- Then revise it.

When you've finished the writing job, take a few minutes to evaluate how the process worked for you. Evaluate especially whether "making holes, not drills," focusing on your purpose, resulted in a more effective message at the end.

3

GET YOUR
STUFF TOGETHER

Manage Your Information

I know it's happened to you. You've bought something that needs assembling—a swing set, a ceiling fan, or a bookcase. An hour's work, tops. But the instructions are badly written, so you don't read them all. Instead, you just start working. Soon you discover that you need a tool or part that you don't have, so work stops while you make a trip to a hardware store. An hour later you're back on the job, and it happens again. Again, you stop work to go buy what you need. The one-hour job stretches into three or four hours.

I know it's happened to you because it's happened to me. And it happens to most of us when we write. As one-stage writers, we jump into writing memos and letters without making sure that we have the materials—the information—that we need. We get halfway into the first paragraph and realize that we need a number from Alice in Accounting, so we stop to call her. In the third paragraph we remember that we need a product description from an online catalogue, so we open a Web browser and find it. As a result of such interruptions, the job takes longer, and the writing is less effective.

If we built houses this way, we'd buy our nails in one little rack package of two or three dozen nails at a time. When we used up each package, we'd stop work to go buy another package. Fortunately, real builders don't work this way. They buy their nails by the box or keg, and they try to buy enough for the whole job before they start driving nails into boards.

That's what we need to do as writers. As much as possible, we need to collect the information we need before we start drafting. Because the decision about what information to include depends on decisions made about your reader(s) and your purpose, collecting information is the third five-minute step in the planning stage of a typical writing hour, as shown in Figure 3-1.

Collecting information as a separate step before you draft has at least four payoffs for you:

1. It reduces interruptions while you're drafting, giving your draft more continuity.
2. It gives you a chance to focus, for a while, *just* on your information. Such focus is crucial, especially if your information includes facts. Executive Donald Walton, in his book *Are You Commu-*

Figure 3-1   Get your stuff together.

Get Your Stuff Together

nicating? said, "The biggest mistake you can make in a report, letter, proposal, or other important message (and it's made all the time) is to write without first getting and correctly analyzing all the facts. It's the one unforgivable mistake. Your boss or customer can overlook a slip in grammar, but not bad advice that results when factual preparation is sloppy and incomplete."

3. It reduces the possibility of omitting important facts or ideas. Unless you systematically capture the facts and ideas you need, they can, as shown in Figure 3-2, easily fall off the conveyor belt of your writing process.

4. It gives you the confidence to draft more easily, with much less anxiety. As long ago as the third century B.C., the Roman statesman Cato the Elder wrote, "Get a grasp on your subject and the words will follow."

ASKING QUESTIONS

The key to getting your stuff together lies in the advice given by Warren Bennis and Burt Nanus in their excellent book on leadership, *Leaders: The Strategies for Taking Charge*: "Successful leaders, we have found, are great askers, and they do pay attention."

Figure 3-2   How your brain loses things along the way.

One "great asker" was Ben Duffy, former head of the great advertising agency Batten, Barton, Durstine and Osborn. According to businessman Peter Hay, Duffy "landed his largest accounts by putting himself into the client's position." Once when Duffy was preparing for a meeting with American Tobacco Company president Vincent Riggio, he listed the questions he would ask if he were in Riggio's shoes, along with the answers he would give in response. According to Hay, "When the time for the interview came, Duffy presented his answers and waited. Riggio reached for a drawer and pulled out a list of questions he had prepared. When he glanced through them he realized that they had all been answered. The two of them went to lunch to celebrate the deal."

To become a great asker yourself, learn to ask "*W/H*" questions, not yes/no questions. That is, ask questions that begin with *Who*, *What*, *Where*, *When*, *Why*, and *How*. Yes/no questions close off further exploration of your topic. *W/H* questions open up possibilities for exploring your topic further.

One great tool for asking questions is the *reporter's checklist*, the set of six *W/H* questions listed in the preceding paragraph. Generations of reporters have learned these questions as a tool for getting the information they need from a source. I learned them from my father, an award-winning editor and publisher of a newspaper in rural Iowa. Whether writing about a town council meeting, a high school basketball game, or a wedding, I needed to be sure to get the *who, what, where, when, why*, and *how* of the event. Business writing is no different. Whenever human beings do something, there are always six *W/H* questions that can be asked and answered. If you ask and answer these questions here at the planning stage, before you begin drafting, you'll be able to draft with less interruption and more continuity. You'll have to make fewer trips back to the store to buy nails.

(Incidentally, the reporter's checklist also can be useful at the revising stage as a check to make sure that you've included essential information. Perhaps a fourth or a third of the meeting announcements and invitations I receive on the job omit the answer to one of the six *W/H* questions and therefore require a follow-up message or phone call.)

Another good list of questions is shown in Figure 3-3. It's my *Four Pairs*. Together, these eight questions can give you eight ways of looking at any subject, ways you otherwise might not have considered. Suppose that you've been asked to research and write a report on a possible supplier. As you look at the first box, "Same," you ask yourself, "How is this supplier like others with whom we've done—or might do—business?" As you look at the next box, "Different," you might ask, "What sets this supplier apart? What is it doing differently from others in this business?"

The next box, "Whole," invites you to think of the supplier's industry: "What are the common elements that run across this business area?" The box headed "Parts" encourages you to ask such questions as, "What is the internal structure of this supplier? Who are the key players?"

As you move to the box headed "Time," you begin to think historically: "How did this company get started? How long has it been around? What have been its ups and downs?" But you also consider time's other direction: "What is the future of this supplier?" The box headed "Space" suggests questions of location and context: "Where is this supplier located? What's the reach of its market?"

The "Cause" box may lead to such questions as, "Why are we considering this supplier? What led us to consider this company?" The box

Figure 3-3 Four pairs of questions.

Same	Different
How is this subject like others?	How is this subject different from others?
Whole	**Parts**
Of what larger whole is this subject a part?	Into what parts can this subject be divided?
Time	**Space**
In what time, or times, does this subject exist?	In what space, or spaces, does this subject exist?
Cause	**Effect**
What is the cause, or causes, of this subject?	What is the effect, or effects, of this subject?
Four Pairs of Questions	

labeled "Effect" might suggest such questions as, "What can go wrong if we enter into a relationship with this supplier? What can go right?"

As I hope you can see, the value of these questions lies in their appropriateness to any subject and in the wealth of further questions they can lead you to. However, don't worry if you can't always get results from all eight boxes. Sometimes the chart will be useful in helping you to come up with just one new angle on your subject. In short, think of the eight questions as prods for brainstorming, and use them to guide you as you jot down all the questions or ideas you can think of.

OUTSIDE AND INSIDE

The information you need for a piece of writing can come from two places:

- Outside of your mind—the stuff you don't know yet
- Inside your mind—the stuff you already know

Sometimes the best source is other people. Particularly for very new or very specialized information, people working in the field will be able to give you answers you can't find in books, magazines, or websites.

Don't be afraid to approach people, even very busy or well-known people, with requests for information. E-mail has made such requests relatively easy to answer. However, also consider phone or face-to-face requests. Because of the possibility of follow-up questions, as well as the nuances that can be conveyed by facial expression and tone of voice, even a very short face-to-face or phone interview can be extremely valuable. When you conduct an interview, consider this advice:

1. **Prepare in advance.** Read what you can find by or about the interviewee, and make a preliminary list of questions you would like answered.
2. **Break the ice.** Take a few seconds to establish a context for the interview and a relationship with the interviewee.

3. **Ask basic *W/H* questions.** Avoid multiple-choice and yes/no questions.

4. **Listen.** Don't be so worried about what your next question will be that you don't hear the answer to the one you've just asked.

5. **Ask follow-up questions.** When points in an answer intrigue or confuse you or suggest whole new lines of inquiry to you, follow up on those points immediately. Don't continue down your list of prepared questions until you've fully explored the answer to each question you've already posed.

6. **Write down what you've learned as soon as possible.** Notes, even recordings, get "cold"; translate them into readable language while they're still warm.

For information from written sources, learn to be a good user of libraries and online resources. The Web has, of course, revolutionized research, and search engines like Google are getting better by the month. However, the Web is the least reliable of sources: it contains both the best and most accurate and the worst and least accurate information. Therefore, use it critically, and try to determine what person or organization is behind the page you're reading.

Be especially careful with Wikipedia. It's a truly wonderful resource, much more comprehensive and up-to-date than any print encyclopedia has ever been. At its best, it's also more accurate than many print sources. But at its worst, it can include information that's just flat-out wrong, put there an hour before by someone who's clueless or misinformed about the subject.

Besides turning to your computer for information, also build an efficient personal library. Keep close to your desk the books and files that you find yourself consulting often. These might include a dictionary, an atlas, and the specialized reference books of your business or profession. Also post prominently at your desk the phone number and Web address of the reference department of your local public or university library. Reference librarians can supply a lot of valuable information for free, over the phone or online.

For "inside" information—the stuff you already know—this step in the planning stage gives you the opportunity to remind yourself of the information you already have and to pull it together into notes or a list. Consider doing some brainstorming in writing: Jot down ideas as quickly as you can, without being concerned about the order they're in or even whether or not you'll use them eventually. At the next step, "Get Your Ducks in a Row" (Chapter 4), you'll have a chance to organize and filter this information.

MAP YOUR INFORMATION

One of my favorite information-gathering tools—a tool I often use at this step of my writing process—is *mind-mapping*. This tool has been popularized widely by Englishman Tony Buzan and American Michael Gelb.

To mind-map, write your main topic or purpose in the center of a large sheet of paper. Perhaps even draw a picture to illustrate it and to engage nonverbal areas of your brain. Then begin drawing branches out from the central topic as subtopics or associations come to mind. Consider doing more drawings, as well as making your map multicolored. In a very short time—well within the five minutes we've allotted to this step in the typical writing hour—you can produce a striking visual aid to use as you continue writing.

Training magazine has reported that the DFS Group, a retailer of luxury goods, has reduced meeting times 40 to 60 percent and trimmed 35 percent off information technology costs by using mind-mapping, supported by the software package MindManager.

Figure 3-4 is a copy of the map I drew using Mindmapper, another excellent piece of software, before I began drafting this chapter. If you compare this map with the resulting chapter, you'll see that my final organization is somewhat different from the organization on the map. But the map certainly served its purpose, helping me survey my topic and make preliminary decisions about what I wanted to include.

Editor and publisher Thomas McCormack said, "Directors, coaches, and editors cannot teach you how to get there. But they can put you

Figure 3-4   Mind map for Chapter 3.

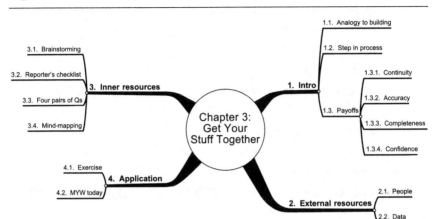

on the paths that lead there." Think of the techniques of this chapter—mind-mapping, brainstorming, the reporter's checklist, interviewing, and others—as paths you can take to find the information you need.

However, whatever paths you take, get your stuff together before you start drafting. Then your one-hour assembly job can actually be done in an hour, with much more effective results.

Exercise

The following questions will test your understanding of this chapter. The final examination for this course will include similar questions.

1. **Why is gathering information the third step in the planning stage?**
    a.   It should be done after defining your community—writer and reader(s)—and after defining your purpose.
    b.   It should be done before organizing the content of your message.
    c.   Both *a* and *b* are true.
    d.   Neither *a* nor *b* is true.

2. **Why should gathering information be done before drafting?**
   a. To reduce interruptions during drafting
   b. To reduce the possibility of leaving out important information
   c. To give you the confidence to draft more easily
   d. All of the above

3. **What kinds of questions are usually best to ask in an interview?**
   a. Yes/no questions
   b. Multiple-choice questions
   c. *Who, what, where, when, why*, and *how* questions
   d. None of the above

4. **The reporter's checklist can be valuable at what stage(s) of the writing process?**
   a. The planning stage
   b. The revising stage
   c. Both *a* and *b*
   d. Neither *a* nor *b*

5. **The Four Pairs of questions for gathering information are based on which of the following sets of words?**
   a. Personality, attitude(s), circumstances, knowledge
   b. Same/different, whole/parts, time/space, cause/effect
   c. *Ko* and *mei*
   d. None of the above

6. **Which of the following is *not* good advice for interviewing?**
   a. Prepare for the interview by reading and by listing questions.
   b. Don't be distracted from your list of questions by the interviewee's responses.
   c. Ask basic *W/H* questions.
   d. Write down what you've learned as soon as possible.

7. **Which of these statements about information on the Web is most true?**
   a. Web-based information is almost always accurate.
   b. Web-information is almost always inaccurate.
   c. Web-based information can be accurate or inaccurate, so it should be read and used critically.
   d. Web-based information can be accurate or inaccurate, so it should not be used.

8. Which of the following is *not* good advice for brainstorming in writing?
   a. Jot down ideas as quickly as you can.
   b. Don't be concerned about the order the ideas are in.
   c. List only those ideas that you're sure you'll use in the piece of writing.
   d. Answers *a, b,* and *c* are all good advice.
9. Which of the following statements about mind-mapping is true?
   a. A mind map should include only the information you'll use in the piece of writing.
   b. A mind map should map information in the order in which it will be used in the piece of writing.
   c. An effective mind map can be done only by computer.
   d. None of these statements is true.
10. Any writing you do at the information-gathering stage should have which of the following characteristics?
   a. It should be carefully spelled and punctuated.
   b. It should be based on your definitions of audience and purpose for the writing job.
   c. It should be carefully organized.
   d. All of the above

MANAGE YOUR WRITING *TODAY*

Now that you've checked your understanding of Chapter 3, you should put it into practice right away.

- On the very next writing job you have to do, begin with some writing management: Remind yourself that you're a writer, that writing can be managed, and that it's largely a matter of managing time. Set up blocks of time for planning, drafting, and revising—with more time allocated for planning and revising than for drafting.
- Then begin the planning stage by "finding the 'we.'" Take perhaps five minutes to ask yourself, "What is the smallest community to which my audience and I both belong?" and "How are my audience and I alike and different in the four PACK dimensions: personality,

attitude, circumstances, and knowledge?" Then take another five minutes to "make holes, not drills" by defining the purpose of the piece of writing. Ask yourself, "Is my purpose to tell my reader(s) about something, ask my reader(s) to do something, or both? Will this piece of writing function as conversation, correspondence, covenant, or conception—or some combination of those?"

- Then practice what you've learned in this chapter, taking as long as you need, at first, to gather information for the piece of writing. Use the reporter's checklist, my Four Pairs, or both. Go to resources, human and written, for the external information you need, and do brainstorming or mind-mapping for the information you already have in your head.
- Next go ahead and do the rest of your planning, thinking about structure. (You'll learn specific organizing methods in the next chapter.)
- Then draft your document with as little editing as possible.
- Take a break.
- Then revise it.

When you've finished the writing job, take a few minutes to evaluate how the process worked for you. Evaluate especially whether "getting your stuff together" in advance resulted in a more effective message at the end.

4

GET YOUR DUCKS IN A ROW

Manage Your Structure

In the first season of the TV series "M*A*S*H," the compound comes under heavy bombardment, but one bomb doesn't explode. Instead, it has nosed its way into the ground in the center of the compound and just sits there—ticking. If it's not defused soon, it will blow up. Frank Burns faints, so Hawkeye Pierce and Trapper John McIntyre are left to defuse the bomb. Colonel Henry Blake gets a copy of the defusing instructions and reads them aloud to Hawkeye and Trapper from behind a sandbag bunker.

"First you need a wrench," he shouts. Hawkeye and Trapper find one. "Place it gently on the nut just above the locking ring and loosen," he continues. They do so. "Now rotate the locking ring counterclockwise." They do.

"Now remove the tail assembly," he reads, "and carefully cut the wires leading to the clockwork fuse at the head." Out come the wire cutters. Snip, snip, . . .

". . . but first, remove the fuse."

Figure 4-1   Writing is linear.

The resulting explosion dramatizes what's perhaps the chief difficulty of putting things in writing: writing is linear. As shown in Figure 4-1, it's made up of one word, phrase, or sentence after another. It's read most often in a "straight line" from beginning to end. Writing is like tape storage for a computer, requiring movement along the line of tape in order to record or access information.

Thought, on the other hand, is usually not linear. When we know something, we know it "all at once" as a network of simultaneous, interconnected ideas, as shown in Figure 4-2. Thought is like a computer's working memory, or RAM, with any information instantly available at any time.

Changing nonlinear thought into linear language is one of the most difficult steps in the writing process. Therefore, this chapter is one of the most important in this book. At this point in the planning stage,

Figure 4-2   Thought is non-linear.

- We have "found the 'we'" by defining our readers and the relationship we have with them.
- We have "made holes, not drills" by defining our purpose in writing.
- We have "gotten our stuff together" by gathering the information we need for the job.

Now we end the planning stage, as shown in Figure 4-3, by "getting our ducks in a row," organizing *this* particular information to achieve *this* particular purpose for *this* particular reader.

The writer of the bomb-defusing instructions knew his subject as a total set of interrelated actions, but he forgot that readers can read only one word, phrase, or sentence at a time. The result was—to say the least—a less-than-effective piece of writing. To be effective, a piece of writing must be organized. It must present its information in the order that best serves the writer's purpose and the reader's needs.

My friend Lee Wood, a former writer at Resort Condominiums International, said that she loves reading documents in which "the writer was so kind as to put himself in my shoes and give me the information in the order I can use it." Most readers are like Lee. A little extra work

Figure 4-3   Get your ducks in a row.

for the writer will save a lot of extra work for the reader—and increase the reader's goodwill.

AN EVERYDAY EXAMPLE

As I mentioned in Chapter 1 when I was talking about the fighter-plane ejection instructions, most of us don't have to write life-and-death instructions every day. However, attention to organization can help even our most routine messages. Consider this memo, which I was given by a client at a Fortune 100 company:

> SUBJECT: Roadway identification in parking lots
> During our Safety Coordinators' meeting the point was made that with our energy conservation program (during the hours of darkness, fog, etc.) roadway identification in our parking lots is hazardous. The recommendation was raised that we might use a fluorescent-type reflecting paint. Would you please investigate the feasibility of this recommendation and advise me as to your decision on implementation?
>
> Your early response is appreciated.

Don't get me wrong. That's not terrible writing. The memo is short enough that it probably will get the job done no matter how it's written. But if you're like most readers I've shown this memo to, you found it difficult to follow. You may even have had to read it twice or three times to understand what it meant. Or you may have given up without understanding.

I'm pretty sure that the writer of this memo was a one-stage writer, as described in the Introduction. I can see her coming from the safety coordinators' meeting, sitting down in front of a keyboard or with a pad of paper, and writing this memo a sentence at a time—planning, drafting, and revising each sentence before moving on to the next one. And like the writer from "M*A*S*H," she seems to have put the information down in the order in which she thought of it, not in the order in which the reader can use it.

The first thing the writer apparently thought of was the meeting she had just left, so she began with that. Then she thought of the problem that was raised at the meeting, the problem she was writing about, so she continued her sentence with that. In the middle of this first sentence she seems to have had a flicker of realization that the relationship between energy conservation and roadway identification might not be clear to her reader, so she interrupted the sentence for a parenthetical explanation. She then thought of the solution that was suggested for the problem, so she wrote a sentence about that. She next thought of what she wanted the reader to do, so she made that her third sentence. Finally, she thought about needing an answer soon, so she made that the last sentence of the memo. Like Allen in Figure 4-4, she simply captured ideas as they came to her. And from her point of view—the writer's point of view—that organization made perfect sense.

From the reader's point of view—*your* point of view in this case— the sense of the memo was probably less than perfect. The first sentence starts with a meeting the reader did not attend and may not even have known about. So already the reader is asking, consciously or subconsciously, WIIFM?—What's in it for me? After the mention of the meet-

Figure 4-4 New ideas rush into Allen's mind pell-mell, crowding old ones out before they take form or shape.

ing, the reader encounters the energy conservation program and then a phrase that looks like an explanation (it's in parentheses, after all), but it doesn't explain anything that's been said so far. Moreover, the parenthetical phrase interrupts the flow of the first sentence, so by the time the reader gets to end of that sentence, he probably has to go back and reread it in order to make sense of it. And even if he does work out what that sentence means, he's still asking, WIIFM?

If the memo were from anybody other than the reader's boss, he might not continue reading. Since it's from his boss, though, he goes on. The second sentence seems to be a response to the point raised in the first sentence, but even so, the WIIFM problem remains. Finally, in the third sentence, the WIIFM question gets answered, in the form of an assignment. The reader's attention perks up at that, so he probably goes back to the beginning again to try to understand what he is being asked to do. In all, from the reader's point of view, reading this short memo has been much more difficult—and annoying—than necessary.

That's why this step in the writing process is so important. As Frank Smith, a leading researcher in the reading process, wrote, "An enormous advantage of writing over speech is that ideas can easily be reorganized in both time and space. They do not have to remain in the order in which they are produced." Here's my suggested revision to the parking lot memo. I don't claim that it's Pulitzer Prize–winning prose, only that it presents information in an order in which the reader can use it—an order more likely to get the results the writer wants:

SUBJECT: Fluorescent paint in parking lots

Can we use fluorescent paint in our parking lots to make traffic lanes easier to see?

    During our Safety Coordinators' meeting, someone pointed out that with our reduced lighting, roadways are hard to see in fog or darkness.

    Please find out whether this solution will work, and let me know within a week.

Thanks.

As you see, this memo begins with what the writer wants the reader to do. And because what the reader is being asked to do is answer a question, the sentence is worded as a question. After reading the first sentence, the reader knows immediately what he's being asked to do: give a yes-or-no answer to a specific query. Then, and only then, is he given the background information that will help him to move toward an answer.

As sports agent Mark H. McCormack wrote, "A lot of memos would be more persuasive if their first and last paragraphs were switched."

THE TECHNIQUE OF ORGANIZING

It's sometimes possible to reorganize a piece of writing, as McCormack implies, at the revising stage of the process. After all, that's the stage at which I reorganized the parking lot memo. But that's a little like changing the floor plan of a house after you've built it. Yes, you could conceivably cut the garage off a completed house and move it to the other end of the building, but that's certainly not the best time to do it. Organizing your information, like laying out the rooms of a house, is best done at the planning stage. As the great twentieth-century philosopher Winnie the Pooh said, "Organizing is what you do before you do something, so that when you do it, it's not all mixed up."

I have deliberately not yet used the dreaded *O* word because I fear that for many readers the word *outline* will call up junior-high memories of Roman numerals, capital letters, Arabic numerals, and lowercase letters all in exactly the right order and spaced and punctuated just right. If you're like me, when you had to turn in a formal outline with your finished paper, you wrote the paper first and then made an outline that matched it. Of course, if you find formal outlines useful for organizing information, by all means use them. But formal outlines certainly aren't necessary at this step in the writing process. For example, when executive Donald Walton talked about the importance of outlining, he clearly meant something pretty informal: "Even if I'm writing something as brief as a one-page letter," he said, "I like to jot down some sort of outline. It may consist of no more than three or four words or phrases: the essence of thought I want to get across and the order in which I intend to build my message."

Walton was right. A good plan at this point in the process may consist of only three or four words or phrases. If you've already jotted down some words or phrases in step 3, then step 4 may consist only of numbering those words or phrases: "Let's see, I'll put this in paragraph 2, this in paragraph 4, this I'll leave out, this in paragraph 1, this also in paragraph 2, this in paragraph 3, and this and this I'll also leave out." If you've made a mind map, you can simply number its branches in the best order for your reader. (In MindManager, you can drag branches around on your screen and then, if you wish, ask the program to number them in clockwise order.)

For most short letters and memos, you may need only a minute or two to decide what information your reader should get first, second, and third. By taking that minute or two to "get your ducks in a row," you'll do your reader a great service. You'll also make the writing process easier for yourself. When you've decided in advance what the main sections of your piece of writing will be and in what order they will come, you won't have to interrupt your drafting to make those decisions. And by dividing your writing task into parts, you'll turn a long, complicated writing job into several shorter, simpler ones. You can then write your letter, memo, or speech one paragraph or section at a time.

For example, as I'm drafting this chapter, next to my computer table is another table with a separate pile of notes for each of the sections I've planned. I gathered those notes in step 3 and arranged them into piles in step 4. Now as I draft, in step 5, all I have to do is go through each pile in order, drafting a section at a time.

FORMULAS

Most writing handbooks devote a lot of space to formulas—prewritten outlines—for organizing various kinds of business writing: job application letters, collection letters, and the like. Don't worry; this book will give you some too. However, it's important to remember that in any business situation, *you* know more than the textbook author. You have defined

- the audience,
- the purpose,
- and the information content

for the particular writing job you have to do, so give yourself credit. After all the careful work you've done in steps 1, 2, and 3, don't just fall back on some textbook formula in step 4. Whether or not you find a formula to base your writing on, you'll be most effective if you ask yourself, "What order should I put *this* particular information in, for *this* purpose, for *this* reader?"

Still, formulas can be helpful as a starting place. Here are four that I find especially useful for requests for information, claims or requests for remedy of a problem, good-news responses to requests, and bad-news responses:

Requests for Information

One of the easiest kinds of business communication is a request for information. Usually no psychological complications come between writer and reader. However, careless organization can make information harder to get. The parking lot memo earlier in this chapter is an example.

When you write a request for information, consider following the plan shown in Figure 4-5. Note that your first paragraph specifically asks for the information you want. If you can put this request in question form, all the better. This will signal more clearly to the reader that you are asking him or her for the answer to this question.

Figure 4-5   Request for information.

Then—and this is important—put in a paragraph break. One important purpose of paragraphing is to signal the major divisions of a piece of writing. A paragraph break after this first question will help to emphasize it.

In your next paragraph or paragraphs, provide any additional information the reader may need. You may not need this paragraph, nor may your reader; that's why it is boxed with dotted lines in the diagram. If your question has several parts, summarize it in the first paragraph, and then, after giving background, break it into a numbered list of specific questions. This numbering will make it easy for your reader to answer your questions without repeating them. He or she can just write, for example:

1. Yes.
2. $13,000.
3. Only if we receive the order by January 1.

The ending of your request will be the last thing your reader reads, so you'll want it to leave a good impression. Avoid flowery, "rubber stamp" endings like "Thank you in advance" or "Begging to remain yours truly." Such endings only sound stilted and phony. If you know your reader well enough to close with a personal reference, by all means do so ("Thanks for your help with the Oswald report, Carmen. I'm glad we're working together again on this one."). Otherwise, a simple "Thanks" or "Thank you" is usually better than a longer, more formal close.

Claims

Claims—requests for the remedy of a problem—require a somewhat different strategy. Making the request in the first sentence may be too abrupt and threatening and so may increase the reader's resistance to solving your problem. A letter that begins "Please repair or replace our Ace-High water cooler immediately" may generate an unnecessarily negative response.

Instead of putting your request first, try putting the problem first, inviting your reader to become an ally instead of an enemy. (When you "found the 'we'" in step 1, you defined a basis for this alliance.) Be clear and forceful, of course, but also give your reader a way to solve your problem while still saving face. For example, you might write the letter this way:

> Our Ace-High water cooler has been giving our water a yellowish color and plastic taste.
>
> We bought the cooler last month under a one-year warranty. The unpleasant color and taste of the water began the first week. We emptied the cooler and washed and rinsed the water bottle thoroughly, but the color and taste have continued.
>
> Will you please repair or replace the cooler as soon as possible? Or if you wish, simply refund its cost.
>
> Thank you.

Try the formula shown in Figure 4-6. In your first paragraph, state the problem and nothing else; this will give your reader the necessary context for the rest of your message. Next, provide background, if necessary. Only then offer a clear solution. When possible, give your reader a choice of acceptable solutions; such a choice will keep your reader from feeling cornered and will increase the chances of compliance. As always, try for a friendly ending.

Figure 4-6   Claim.

Figure 4-7   Good-news response.

Good-News Responses

Giving your reader good news is like rowing downstream with a wind at your back: you have everything going for you. Therefore, as shown in Figure 4-7, begin with the good news so that your reader will recognize it immediately and be pleased by it. Begin, perhaps, with the word *yes*. The word *you* is a good second choice. Then insert a paragraph break as a way of emphasizing the good news.

The following paragraph(s), if necessary, should carry any qualifications. These should never constitute a retreat from the good news, such as "Yes, you will receive the raise you requested at such time as it can be accurately determined that hell has frozen over."

The closing paragraph should be a friendly ending, but remember, not a rubber-stamp one.

Bad-News Responses

When you have to give bad news, you naturally have a much harder job. You are rowing upstream, against the current of the reader's attitude. Therefore, consider beginning, as shown in Figure 4-8, with a neutral statement establishing the context for the response.

Then move to the reasons or process that led to the negative decision. Finally, state the bad news, but follow it immediately with a goodwill

Figure 4-8   Bad-news response.

message. If this message can offer the reader something as a compromise, all the better.

When you have bad news to give, nothing you can do as a writer will guarantee the reader's goodwill. However, by organizing your message carefully, you can at least increase the probability that your reader will read and understand the reasons for the bad news.

WRITING TO SELL

When I asked more than a hundred business leaders, "What are your three biggest communication problems?" the number two answer (after "speaking to a group") was "being persuasive." These leaders recognized that the essence of business is persuading people to buy. And the essence of leadership is having a vision, communicating it to others, and influencing them to follow. Effective communicators need to know how to change minds.

When your purpose is to persuade your reader to buy—buy your product, service, ideas, or vision—you can use either of two basic strategies: direct or indirect. Direct persuasion dates from ancient Greece and is based on the assumption that your reader is a reasonable person who will be persuaded by good reasons. In direct persuasion, you simply state your position and then list reasons for it.

If you have written school papers that were based on a *thesis statement*, you have used direct persuasion in writing. A thesis statement is simply a statement of a position, which is then supported by reasons in the rest of a paper. The following first paragraph of a letter to a U.S. senator ends with a traditional thesis statement, which the rest of the letter goes on to support.

> As you know, the U.S. government has been purchasing dairy cattle from farmers since the middle of 1986. In my opinion, the whole-herd dairy buyout program, as it is called, was a mistake.

Indirect persuasion is also ancient in its use, but it has not been taught formally until recently. It is based on the assumption that your reader may have an opposing position that he or she may not easily give up. Efforts to confront such a reader directly may lead not to successful persuasion but to a hardening of the reader's original position. Therefore, indirect persuasion attempts to gain the reader's acceptance by creating an atmosphere of cooperation and mutual understanding.

Abraham Lincoln was talking about indirect persuasion when he said, "If you would win a man to your cause, first convince him that you are his sincere friend."

To persuade indirectly, begin by stating the problem objectively and, especially, stating the opposing position accurately. By doing so, you demonstrate that you are a fair person who can see things through your opponents' eyes. Having done this, you can even go a step further, stating the circumstances in which your opponents' position is, in fact, the right one.

At this point your relationship with your reader should be firmly established, so you can safely proceed to state your position and the circumstances in which it is the correct one.

Notice that you have not threatened or alienated your reader by opposing his or her position. Instead, you have agreed with it, at least in certain circumstances. All you have done is shown that circumstances also exist in which *your* position is right.

With this balance established between the two positions, you can then go ahead to tip the balance your way by showing that the circumstances in which your position is the right one are the circumstances that exist now. Better still, sometimes you can present your position as simply a desirable modification of the opposing one. Or you can suggest a combination of both positions as the best solution.

Here's an example of indirect persuasion:

> Thank you for asking me to comment on Dwight's proposal that Casey and Evans begin direct mail-order sales of our product line. The proposal obviously has been thought out carefully; it includes impressive statistics on the profit potential of mail-order sales and a detailed plan for building a mailing list and handling the shipment of orders.
>
> The proposal is a sound one. In these days of two-income families and busy schedules, consumers are finding it increasingly convenient to shop by mail. Moreover, the mail-order companies that have earned high brand-name recognition are enjoying the benefits of direct marketing.
>
> However, new companies just entering the mail-order industry—companies without existing recognition and reputation—are not doing well. Given the state of the economy and the high prices for printing and postage, this is not a good time for such companies to begin mail-order sales.
>
> Unfortunately, Casey and Evans is such a company; while we have a reputation among retailers for quality novelty items, that recognition does not extend to the consumer. I suggest, therefore, that Dwight's excellent proposal be postponed until economic conditions improve. Meanwhile, Casey and Evans should begin to give our brand name greater prominence on our products. I believe that in the future we might well want to move into mail-order sales.

Whichever strategy you adopt, keep in mind the basic principles of persuasion. Psychologist Robert B. Cialdini, after 30 years of research into what makes people comply with requests, identified six human tendencies that can lead to compliance:

1. **Reciprocation.** People are more likely to give you something if they get something back.
2. **Consistency.** If people comply with one request, they are more likely to comply with others.
3. **Social validation.** People are more likely to comply if others are complying.
4. **Liking.** People are more likely to comply with requests from people they like.
5. **Authority.** People are more likely to comply with requests from people they see as being in authority.
6. **Scarcity.** People are likely to comply with requests when they see what they will receive as scarce.

FROM INFORMATION TO KNOWLEDGE

Remember that the first sentence of this book referred to the *knowledge economy*. I prefer that to the terms *information age* and *information economy* because information by itself has little or no value. To be valuable, information must be *organized* and *communicated* and thus turned into knowledge.

Futurist John Naisbitt, in his visionary book *Megatrends*, wrote, "We are drowning in information but starved for knowledge." Software entrepreneur Neil Larson offered the solution: "Knowledge is information with structure." Similarly, knowledge management guru Thomas A. Stewart said, "Intelligence becomes an asset when some useful order is created out of free-floating brainpower." And corporate VP Jim Roe wrote, "If you are writing to give information, you are wasting your time and the reader's. We are being buried in useless information. The Internet and mass publications flood us with information. Corporations send out reams of information to us via email, faxes, computer reports, and pamphlets. 99.9 percent of it is useless to me. I do not seek information. I seek knowledge that I can convert to understanding and then, hopefully, to wisdom."

So when you spend five minutes or so on step 4, "getting your ducks in a row," you're doing much more than a writing exercise. You're converting information into knowledge, intelligence into an asset. You're helping solve a piece of your reader's information-overload problem. You are truly creating value in a knowledge economy.

Exercises

Exercise A

The following questions will test your understanding of this chapter. The final examination for this course will include similar questions.

1. Why is organizing information the fourth step in the planning stage?
   a. It should be done after defining your community, defining your purpose, and gathering your information.
   b. It should be done before drafting your message.
   c. Both *a* and *b* are true.
   d. Neither *a* nor *b* is true.
2. Why should organizing be done before drafting?
   a. To reduce interruptions during drafting
   b. To allow you to focus on the best order for the reader
   c. To turn the drafting job into a series of smaller jobs
   d. All the above
3. Which of the following is a common difficulty with writing?
   a. It requires converting linear thinking into nonlinear writing.
   b. It requires converting nonlinear thinking into linear writing.
   c. It requires converting static thinking into active writing.
   d. None of the above

4. **Which of the following is/are characteristic(s) of one-stage writers?**
   a. They write in the order they think of things.
   b. They write in the most effective order for the reader.
   c. Both *a* and *b*
   d. Neither *a* nor *b*

5. **Should formal outlines be used at the planning stage?**
   a. Yes, they should always be used.
   b. No, they should never be used.
   c. They should be used only if they are useful to the writer.
   d. They should be used only when writing speeches.

6. **Unless you have a good reason otherwise, how should routine requests for information begin?**
   a. With background information
   b. With the request itself, phrased as a question if possible
   c. With friendly, personal information
   d. With the reason for the request

7. **Unless you have a good reason otherwise, how should claims begin?**
   a. With background information
   b. With the request itself, phrased as a question if possible
   c. With friendly, personal information
   d. With a statement of the problem

8. **Unless you have a good reason otherwise, how should good-news responses begin?**
   a. With background information
   b. With the good news
   c. With friendly, personal information
   d. With any qualifications about the good news

9. **Unless you have a good reason otherwise, how should bad-news responses begin?**
   a. With background information
   b. With the bad news
   c. With an acknowledgment of the request
   d. With any qualifications about the bad news

10. Which of the following is *not* a feature of indirect persuasion?
    a. It begins with a clear statement of your position.
    b. It begins with a clear statement of the problem.
    c. It acknowledges and clearly states your opponents' position(s).
    d. It describes the circumstances in which your opponents' position is correct.

Exercise B

You are a tax accountant. One of your clients is Dr. Barbara Smith, a retired university professor. Recently, she received a letter from the Internal Revenue Service (IRS) proposing that her latest tax return was incorrect.

You are writing a response to the IRS and have listed the following facts. Number the facts in the order you would include them in your letter.

_____   The IRS claims that three payments to Dr. Smith were not listed as income on her tax return.

_____   The letter from the IRS was headed "Proposed Changes to Income" and was dated December 2, _____.

_____   The Teachers Insurance and Annuity Association payment was $1,213. Of this amount, $516 was reported on Schedule B as dividends.

_____   The College Retirement Equity annuity of $2,656 indeed appears to have been omitted from the return.

_____   Dr. Smith operates a business that includes writing.

_____   Of the Teachers Insurance and Annuity Association payment, $697 was reported on line 16 as fully taxable pension.

_____   You want the IRS to send Dr. Smith a revised tax bill.

_____   Dr. Smith's Social Security number is _____.

_____   The book royalties of $275 were included in the $4,660 gross receipts on Schedule C as business income.

MANAGE YOUR WRITING *TODAY*

Now that you've checked your understanding of Chapter 4, you should put it into practice right away.

- On the very next writing job you have to do, begin with some writing management: Remind yourself that you're a writer, that writing can be managed, and that it's largely a matter of managing time. Set up blocks of time for planning, drafting, and revising—with more time allocated for planning and revising than for drafting.
- Then begin the planning stage by "finding the 'we.'" Take perhaps five minutes to ask yourself, "What is the smallest community to which my audience and I both belong?" and "How are my audience and I alike and different in the four PACK dimensions: personality, attitude, circumstances, and knowledge?"
- Then take another five minutes to "make holes, not drills" by defining the purpose of the piece of writing. Ask yourself, "Is my purpose to tell my reader(s) about something, ask my reader(s) to do something, or both? Will this piece of writing function as conversation, correspondence, covenant, or conception—or some combination of those?"
- Take another five minutes or so to gather information for the piece of writing. Use the reporter's checklist, my Four Pairs, or both. Go to human and written resources for the external information you need, and do brainstorming or mind-mapping for the information you already have in your head.
- Next spend as much time as you need on organizing this information to best achieve your purpose for your reader(s). If your writing task is a request for information, claim, or good-news or bad-news response, begin with one of the formulas in this chapter. If your task is persuasion, decide whether to use direct or indirect persuasion. Make whatever kind of outline or numbered list works for you.

- Then draft your document with as little editing as possible.
- Take a break.
- Then revise it.

When you've finished the writing job, take a few minutes to evaluate how the process worked for you. Evaluate especially whether "getting your ducks in a row" in advance resulted in a more effective piece of writing at the end.

DO IT WRONG
THE FIRST TIME

Manage Your Drafting

W e've finished the planning stage of the writing process, so we're ready to draft. We've defined our reader(s), defined our purpose, gathered our information, and decided how to organize that information. Now, at the drafting stage, it's time to actually write the document for the first time.

As you've seen, this step is "Do It Wrong the First Time." In this age of Zero Defects, Total Quality Management, Six Sigma, and ISO-whatever, this advice may seem like heresy. However, as Ken Blanchard and Robert Lorber wrote in *Putting the One Minute Manager to Work*, "Anything worth doing does not have to be done perfectly—at first." Remember that, as Figure 5-1 shows, we're only about 25 minutes into the typical writing hour. We can afford to make mistakes now in the interest of a better result at the end. We'll have time later to make the document perfect.

Figure 5-1   Do it wrong the first time.

Great novelists have always known the benefit of doing it wrong the first time. William Faulkner advised, "Get it down. Take chances. It may be bad, but it's the only way you can do anything really good." And Bernard DeVoto wrote, "The best reason for putting anything down on paper is that one may then change it." We business writers can learn from them.

DRAFT AS PROTOTYPE

I learned the reason for doing it wrong the first time not from novelists but from a group of managers I was training at a manufacturing site of a Fortune 100 company. Our training room was lined with motivational posters proclaiming such principles as "Think," "Quality Comes First," and yes, "Do It Right the First Time." My group of managers quickly challenged my directive to "Do It Wrong the First Time." I realized that these managers saw me as just a crazy consultant from outside who was clueless about their strong quality-oriented corporate culture.

For once, I realized what to do. The plant where I was working made printers, so I asked the managers to tell me the story of how their company developed and manufactured a new printer model.

Well, they said, we put together a planning team from a variety of specialties. There's a marketer who talks about what will sell next year.

There's an engineer who lets the team know what new technologies are available. There's a money person who brings a budget framework for the project. And so on. Together they begin envisioning the new printer. As they work, more engineers are brought in to convert the team's vision into more and more detailed blueprints.

And then, the managers said, these high-priced designers turn the blueprints over to Charlie. And Charlie goes into his shop and actually builds the printer. Charlie has to form a sheet-metal case manually, of course. And because he may not have the integrated circuits yet, he may have to do some hard-wiring. But before long, the first printer is made.

At this point in their story, I interrupted. "So Charlie makes sure to put the company's nameplate on that first printer?" I asked. "And he stamps it with serial number 1? Because you're eventually going to sell it, right?"

The managers laughed. "Of course not," they said. "The printer that Charlie builds is just a *prototype*. It's not built to sell; it's built just to test."

"Ah ha!" I gloated. "So you don't do it right the first time. Because you know you won't sell the prototype, it doesn't have to be perfect. Making it perfect—with the right nameplate and paint and all—would be a huge waste of time and would distract you from the more important features that have to be tested."

Now please understand that such flashes of insight are rare for me. But this time the managers helped me arrive at an insight that worked for them—and has worked for me ever since. When a company develops a new product, it doesn't worry about making the first one perfect, as if it will be sold to a customer. The first one or two—probably even the first one or two dozen—are prototypes, built for testing and refining. Building and testing these imperfect prototypes are important steps toward finally "doing it right."

However, that's not how most of us write. We try to skip the prototype stage and go right to the final product. Most of us edit carefully as we write, pausing every few words to check spelling or punctuation or grammar. But as novelist Robert Cormer said, "The beautiful part of writing is that you don't have to get it right the first time, unlike, say, a brain surgeon."

A draft is a prototype. It's not the final product. It's not written for the reader, it's written for the writer. It's "quick and dirty." It's written to test. It's written to see if it does what it was planned to do.

David William Peace, a reader of my blog, commented, "I tell my wife (after telling her how much I wrote today) that I just keep writing to the point of thinking I am done, and then pick the pen back up and keep writing. Also, I try to convey my motto in writing the first draft: No one is going to see your mistakes. Who cares if anyone did? Very few people will bother putting forth the effort. I am now addicted to writing without thinking on a daily basis."

When you move from the planning to the drafting stage, you do so because you can't plan the document anymore. As author Natalie Goldberg has said, "Finally, one just has to shut up, sit down, and write." You just have to build a prototype to see if it works. In doing so, you're following the lead of management guru Tom Peters. "On the wall of my Vermont writing studio," he wrote, "is a quote by David Kelley, founder of IDEO Product Design: 'Fail faster. Succeed sooner.' Next to it hangs a saying by the extraordinary photographer Diane Arbus, who told her students: 'Learn not to be careful.'"

Exercise

This chapter won't contribute any questions to the final examination. However, the exercise in this chapter is one of the most important in the course, so please do it.

- Find a 10-minute time period when you probably won't be interrupted. Turn off your cell phone. If you're at work and you have an office with a door, close it. Put up a sticky note that says, "Do not disturb." If you're at home, ask your family not to interrupt you for 10 minutes.

- Then, if you can type faster than you can write by hand, open a new document in your word processing program. If you can write faster by hand, grab a smooth-writing pen and a couple of fresh sheets of paper.
- Notice the time, and then start writing. Write for 10 minutes as fast as you physically can, literally without stopping. Write "quick and dirty." Don't stop to think of what to say next. (If you have to, just write, "I don't know what to write. I don't know what to write. . . ." until you think of something to write.) Don't stop to read what you've written. Don't stop to correct spelling, punctuation, or grammar. Don't stop to change anything. (If you need to, turn off your computer monitor or turn its brightness all the way down.) In short, follow novelist John Steinbeck's advice: "Write freely and as rapidly as possible and throw the whole thing on paper. Never correct or rewrite until the whole thing is down."
- After 10 minutes, just stop.

DEBRIEFING THE EXERCISE

At the end of the 10 minutes, you may not have Pulitzer Prize–winning prose, but you'll have achieved two things:

1. You've probably produced more writing than you've ever generated before in 10 minutes. According to language specialist Frank Smith, we can produce language, in the form of speech, at about 250 words a minute. A keyboard might slow us down to 50 words per minute. However, even at the snail's pace of keyboarding or handwriting, the 5 minutes we've arbitrarily allocated for drafting should give us time to produce 250 words—all we need for a one-hour letter or memo. All of us can, in fact, write much faster than we normally do as long as we don't plan or revise while we're drafting.

2. You've experienced what it can feel like to write without editing. You may not have felt comfortable at first because there may have been a part of you that kept wanting to stop to fix things. (In the next chapter we'll talk about that part of you. We'll even give it a name.)

However, perhaps by the end of the 10 minutes you began to feel more comfortable. You may have experienced what writer Richard Andersen called "get[ting] out of the words' way."

In a real situation, of course, you will have prepared for this quick and dirty draft by asking some important questions about your reader, purpose, subject matter, and organization. In short, you will have done the planning taught so far in this course. Even in a real situation, though, you can then draft virtually without stopping. If you don't know how to spell a word, you can just approximate; you or your spell-checker can fix it later. If you don't know which of two words to use, you can use them both; you can decide between them when you look at your draft again at the revising stage. For now, you just need to get comfortable with doing it wrong the first time. As the great editor Maxwell Perkins said, "Just get it down on paper, and then we'll see what to do with it."

You see, in the long run, stopping to edit while we draft breaks our train of thought and keeps us from being as smart or creative as we could be. Moreover, it commits us much too early to the illusion of perfection, keeping us from doing the later revision that could help our writing get its job done better. In the long run, getting it "right" the first time keeps us from communicating as effectively as we could. Our communication and our careers suffer.

Comedy writer Larry Gelbart said it well: "You have to allow yourself the liberty of writing poorly. You have to get the bulk of it done, and then you start to refine it. You have to put down less than marvelous material just to keep going to whatever you think the end is going to be—which may be something else altogether by the time you get there."

OVERCOMING WRITER'S BLOCK

Journalist Gene Fowler once wrote, "Writing is easy; all you do is sit staring at a blank sheet of paper until the drops of blood form on your forehead." While most of us haven't literally had that experience, I suspect that most of us have suffered, like Cynthia in Figure 5-2, from writer's block.

Figure 5-2   Cynthia comes face to face with the possibility that brains may be self-cleaning.

In my experience—and in the experience of many writers I've worked with—writer's block is usually the result of fear. As James Wal-droop, cofounder of the consulting firm Peregrine Partners, said, "The enemy of a good decision is fear—fear of failure, fear of humiliation, fear of making a mistake."

The best way I know to get past that fear is to just start writing, while giving yourself permission to do it wrong the first time. If it helps, write yourself an e-mail about why you can't get started writing. Before you know it, you're writing.

To overcome writer's block, follow Frank Smith's advice: "Do not expect the writing to come out right the first time. Do not be afraid of the possibility that what you write will fail to live up to your expectations, or those of the schoolteacher on your shoulder. Anything you write can be changed. Anything you write can be thrown away. You have nothing to lose."

WRITING AND "FLOW"

One way to understand the benefits of quick and dirty drafting—and of five-stage writing as a whole process—is based on the work of psychologist Mihaly Csikszentmihalyi (pronounced "chick sent me HIGH"). He observed that all human experiences provide varying degrees of challenge. For example, the experience of making toast for breakfast presents a fairly low level of challenge, whereas the experience of preparing a full Chinese banquet presents a higher level of challenge.

We meet life's challenges, said Csikszentmihalyi, with varying degrees of skill. A novice Chinese chef brings to the banquet preparation a relatively low level of skill; a veteran chef brings a much higher level.

Csikszentmihalyi wrote that if the challenge presented by an experience exceeds our skill, the result is anxiety, as shown in Figure 5-3. A novice chef faced with the preparation of an entire banquet will be understandably anxious. If, on the other hand, our skill exceeds the challenge, the result is boredom. The master chef forced to make toast all day will soon become bored.

If skill and challenge are more or less evenly matched, however, the result is what Csikszentmihalyi calls "flow," the state of being totally engrossed in the experience. Experiences that provide flow are the experiences we tend to do for their own sake. Ronald Gross, in his book *Peak Learning*, called the anxiety state the "groan zone" and the boredom state the "drone zone," as contrasted with the "flow zone."

Csikszentmihalyi and his fellow researchers looked at many kinds of flow-producing experiences, from chess to rock climbing to surgery,

Figure 5-3   Flow.

and identified eight "characteristic dimensions" of the flow experience. Csikszentmihalyi's book *The Evolving Self* lists these eight characteristics as follows:

1. Clear goals: an objective is distinctly defined; immediate feedback: one knows instantly how well one is doing.
2. The opportunities for acting decisively are relatively high, and they are matched by one's perceived ability to act. In other words, personal skills are well suited to given challenges.
3. Action and awareness merge; one-pointedness of mind.
4. Concentration on the task at hand; irrelevant stimuli disappear from consciousness, worries and concerns are temporarily suspended.
5. A sense of potential control.
6. Loss of self-consciousness, transcendence of ego boundaries, a sense of growth and of being part of some greater entity.
7. Altered sense of time, which usually seems to pass faster.
8. Experience becomes autotelic: If several of the previous conditions are present, what one does becomes autotelic, or worth doing for its own sake.

The planning stage of the five-stage process gives you dimension 1—clear goals. By the time you start your quick and dirty draft, you have a clearly defined objective for that draft, as well as a clear set of criteria to use during the revising stage. The fact that writing begins with a blank page gives you dimension 2—the opportunity for acting decisively by using the best of your skills. The law of the next action provides dimensions 3 and 4—"one-pointedness" of mind and concentration on the task at hand. By dividing your writing process into 12 distinctive steps, you can focus intently on each one as you move through it. At the drafting stage, for example, you focus only on getting words down, not on getting them right. If you've taken time in step 1 to define yourself as a writer, you'll have achieved dimension 5—a sense of potential control. Together, dimensions 3 and 4 can get you to dimensions 6 and 7—a loss of self-consciousness and an altered sense of time. By the end of your 10-minute drafting exercise, you may have already experienced these dimensions. In all, therefore, a five-stage writing process can achieve dimension 8 by making writing an autotelic experience for you—a satisfying "flow" experience that can be enjoyed for its own sake.

MANAGE YOUR WRITING *TODAY*

In this chapter's exercise, you practiced quick and dirty drafting—drafting without editing. Now it's time to do it for real.

- On the very next writing job you have to do, begin with some writing management: Remind yourself that you're a writer, that writing can be managed, and that it's largely a matter of managing time. Set up blocks of time for planning, drafting, and revising—with more time allocated for planning and revising than for drafting.
- Then begin the planning stage by "finding the 'we.'" Take perhaps five minutes to ask yourself, "What is the smallest community to which my audience and I both belong?" and "How are my audience and I alike and different in the four PACK dimensions: personality, attitude, circumstances, and knowledge?" Then take another five minutes to "make holes, not drills" by defining the purpose of the piece of writing. Ask yourself, "Is my purpose to tell my reader(s) about something, ask my reader(s) to do something, or both? Will this piece of writing function as conversation, correspondence, covenant, or conception—or some combination of those?" Take another five minutes or so to "get your stuff together," to gather information for the piece of writing. Use the reporter's checklist, my Four Pairs, or both. Go to human and written resources for the external information you need, and do brainstorming or mind-mapping for the information you already have in your head. Then end the planning stage with five minutes of "getting your ducks in a row," organizing your information to best achieve your purpose for your reader(s).
- Next "do it wrong the first time." Draft your document with as little editing as possible. Consider turning off your computer monitor as

you do so. Remember horror writer Stephen King's admonishment that "Only God gets it right the first time."

- Then take a break.
- When you come back from the break, revise your document.

When you've finished, take a few minutes to evaluate how the process worked for you. Evaluate especially whether "doing it wrong the first time" resulted in a more effective piece of writing at the end.

As Bradley S. Hayden of Western Michigan University said, "Drafts are like newly born children: We can't expect them to go to graduate school when they are only a few days old. The most important thing is for them to have arrived into the world safely."

6

TAKE A BREAK AND CHANGE HATS
Manage Your Internal Writer and Editor

I n the introduction to this book you learned the importance of improving your written products by improving your writing process. Specifically, you learned the importance of becoming a five-stage writer. In Chapters 1 through 4 you learned specific tools for the planning stage of the process.

Now, as shown in Figure 6-1, you've come to what may be the most important stage in the writing process—the "down" time, the time you're not writing. Although you may have trouble justifying this to your boss or to your spouse, it's true. This important stage is the time between drafting and revising when you should get away from your writing—for minutes, for hours, or (if possible) for days. It's the time to take a break and change hats. We professional business writers—especially we older ones—even have a technical term for this stage. We call it "Miller Time."

Figure 6-1   Take a break and change hats.

Take a Break and
Change Hats

BREAKING FOR OBJECTIVITY

Let's take the two parts of this chapter's title one part at a time. First is "Take a Break."

The reason for taking a break after drafting is that it can give you the "distance"—the objectivity—that you need to do good revision. Objectivity is important for at least three reasons.

The first, and most basic, reason is that objectivity lets you see what you wrote, not what you may have meant to write. Ask any writing teacher or trainer, and he or she will confirm the fact that many developing writers will look at their draft and literally read what they intended to say, not what they actually said. Once I worked with a writer who read aloud to me a sentence from his draft four times before realizing his mistake, exclaiming, "Duh!" and reading the sentence the way it was written on the page. You can't revise something until you've actually seen it.

The second reason is that objectivity will help you to see the document as the reader will see it. In 1751, the Earl of Chesterfield advised his son, "Read every paragraph after you have written it, in the critical view of discovering whether it is possible that any one man can mistake the true sense of it: and correct it accordingly."

The memo in Chapter 4 about the use of fluorescent paint in parking lots was easily understandable by the writer. She knew exactly what she wanted to say. Even though she had not organized it carefully at the planning stage, she could have reorganized it at the revising stage if she had gotten some distance from it and read it from her reader's point of view. Before you revise a draft, you need to read it as if for the first time—the way your reader(s) will encounter it.

The third, and perhaps most important, reason for objectivity is that it can help you to overcome your own ego. Even if you don't think of yourself as a good writer, you feel close to the bad writing you've done. You don't want to accept criticism, even from yourself.

Once you've written a draft, you've invested quite a bit of time and effort in it. Thus, as Rabbi Israel Salanter said, "Writing is one of the easiest things; erasing is one of the hardest." You may be reluctant to admit, even to yourself, that something you've drafted might benefit from being changed.

Have you ever had the experience of reading a piece of writing that you did as a child or adolescent? Perhaps you've found old school papers, or love letters, or a diary. In my own experience, reading my oldest writing is both embarrassing and fun—because the writing sounds as if it were written by a totally different person. And of course, it was.

As I'm sitting here preparing the second edition of this book, I'm revising sentences and paragraphs that I first wrote more than five years ago. I'm a different person from the one I was then. I hope I've learned from another five years' experience as a businessman and writer.

In business, of course, you don't have the luxury of waiting 5, 10, or 20 years to read your draft again. So you have to force yourself to get something of the same kind of distance, the same kind of objectivity. Even in five minutes you can trick yourself. You can print out your quick and dirty draft, set it down without reading it, and head for the restroom, vending machine, or coffee pot. When you return, you can say to yourself, "Oh, there's that sales letter I've been putting off writing. Look! Someone must have drafted it for me! Hmm, let me read it. Well, it's not bad—but it's certainly not up to my standards yet. I'm not willing to put my name on it now. But at least it's been written! All I have to do is revise it until it's good enough for my signature."

Remember: The draft is a prototype, it's not a finished product. It's raw material.

In a way, writing is like poker. In poker, it's important not to think of any of the money in the pot as your money. If you put $10 in the pot before the draw, you just have to forget that fact. If, after the draw, you keep thinking of that $10 as yours, you'll be betting to protect your investment—and you'll make bad decisions. There's even a phrase from poker that applies to how writers should treat a first draft: "Don't throw good money after bad."

Poker, writing—the principle is the same. If you think of the time and effort you've invested in a piece of writing, you're bound to be reluctant to change anything. However, to be an effective business writer, you simply have to lose that reluctance. As Nikole Gipps of NHG Consulting has written, "Don't create an emotional attachment to your business writing." And poet John Berryman said, "One must be ruthless with one's own writing or someone else will be."

When I tell you to take a five-minute break out of a typical writing hour, that's the minimum. To the extent that you can control your time, if you have two days to do a one-hour piece of writing, complete your planning and drafting stages the first day and save your revising until the second day. Sports agent Mark H. McCormack reminded us that "whenever President Harry Truman wrote an angry letter, he would put it away in his desk for 24 hours to see if he felt the same way the next day." Even with nonangry documents, a 24-hour break can be hugely valuable.

If you have a week, putting four days between drafting and revising almost certainly will make your document stronger. And if you're lucky enough to have more time, use it!

There's one more important strategy for getting the objectivity you need to revise effectively. I've been talking so far about the value of *pretending* that someone else wrote the draft. What if someone else really *did*? Consider setting up an underground, subversive writing team in which you and a coworker routinely revise each other's drafts. You'll both end up writing better—and looking better.

FROM WRITER-BASED TO READER-BASED

One phenomenon that often happens when writers take a break and become more objective about their drafts is that they move from what theorist Linda Flower calls "writer-based" writing to what she calls "reader-based" writing. Writer-based writing is simply a record of the writer's own thought, with no concessions to the needs of a reader.

For an example of writer-based writing, read the following paragraphs of a memo from the vice president for human resources at one of my client companies, a large insurance firm:

> I received the results from the Spring examinations. I want to extend my congratulations to you for your success in passing Parts I and II. I know that to achieve this success took a special effort on your part.
>
> I am pleased that you are interested in your personal development and have taken the initiative to improve your knowledge of the insurance business and to increase your value to the company.

That's not bad for a quick and dirty draft. But when the vice president took a break and looked at the draft objectively, he realized that the memo was very writer-based. Each of its four sentences had *I* as its grammatical subject, as if the most important information in the message was that the vice president thought and felt something. Such self-centeredness doesn't necessarily reveal a massive ego problem; it's actually quite typical of first drafts.

Although such writer-centered writing is usually not effective at getting things done, Flower believed that it may be a necessary step in the writing process. Writers, she said, may need to first get words on paper (or on a computer screen) and only then shape them to meet the reader's needs. Here's how the vice president reshaped the memo to change its emphasis:

Congratulations on passing Parts I and II of the Spring examinations. Your success reflects a special effort on your part.

Your interest in your personal development and the initiative to improve your knowledge of the insurance business certainly increase your value to the company.

Although these sentences could still use some revision, they certainly show an effective move from writer-based to reader-based writing.

In the drafting stage, even with good planning, language may be spun out from the writer's mind organically, like silk from a silkworm. Before the revising stage can start, that language needs to become objective, like silk thread that can be woven into something beautiful, like a scarf, or useful, like a parachute.

This "weaving" process requires a special kind of double vision. On one hand, the writer must see the written document as a whole, just as a silk weaver must see the overall pattern of the fabric emerging from the loom. But the writer also must see the document as a collection of individual parts that can be manipulated, just as the weaver must concentrate on the individual threads of the warp and woof. Weavers do not have a problem achieving this double vision, nor do architects, thinking both of grand sweeps of space and of individual beams and panes of glass. Yet we writers often have trouble seeing our work in this dual fashion.

One reason lies in economics. We writers generate our material out of ourselves, so we come to value it as we would a child—and a child born of an especially hard labor. Moreover, we writers know instinctively the almost infinite power of the written word—the power, as mentioned in the introduction, of creating a reality. Words, to us, become almost sacred, priceless things.

Yet, to be good writers, we also must come to regard words as cheap, among the cheapest commodities on earth. We must know that the writing of a word takes only a second or two and a fraction of a penny's worth of electricity or ink—and that erasing that word costs even less. And we must be willing to do that erasing, that total destruction of language, without even a flicker of regret. In short, we must learn not to undervalue—or overvalue—the written word.

A *Time* article, in lamenting "The Decline of Editing," quoted writer John McPhee: "There are a lot of books around that smell of the tape recorder. Writing is so difficult that if a writer is looking at words on paper, say the transcript of a tape recording, it's damn difficult to resist them." The result, claimed McPhee, is wordiness: "A lot of books go on too long because [the writer] recorded too much."

We can all learn from novelist and playwright Thornton Wilder. "An incinerator," he said, "is a writer's best friend."

THE TWO HATS

The second part of this chapter's title is "Change Hats." That's because we businesspeople wear two hats when we write. And trying to wear both at the same time keeps us from writing as powerfully as we could.

You see, two different mental activities are involved in the writing process. (I'll sometimes refer to them as two different parts of the brain, although that's not exactly true.)

One of these activities—occupying a big part of the brain—is the unbelievably complex job of converting ideas into hand movements. Think for a moment about what a complicated activity that is. You're at your computer, writing up your travel expenses and remembering the blue sedan you rented at O'Hare Airport to get you around town. Your brain moves some muscles in the middle finger of your left hand, then the little finger, and then the index finger. The word *car* appears on the screen.

I think of that part of my brain as a tough-guy big-city reporter from black-and-white B movies of the 1930s, '40s, and '50s, able to pound out an article at a moment's notice—the hard-boiled newsman who says, "Give me the story, chief, and I'll do it." I call that part of my brain my *Internal Writer*—and imagine him in a rumpled fedora with a press card in the hatband.

But psychologists tell us that another mental activity is also involved. It occupies the part of your brain that remembers the sedan and knows where you put the charge slip. It's the part that knows how expense reports look and what you can include in them. It's the part that also knows all those grammar and punctuation rules.

I think of that part of my brain as a crusty old newspaper editor from those same movies, yelling out assignments to his staff and grabbing the pencil from behind his ear to slash up the stories they submit. I call that part of my brain my *Internal Editor*—and picture him in a green eyeshade.

Now imagine that you're a newspaper reporter on your first day at work. Your boss gives you a wire story from the Associated Press and asks you to rewrite it. You sit down at your keyboard and start writing your first sentence. Suddenly you hear your boss's voice over your shoulder: "What a lousy way to start a story," he says.

"How do you want me to start it?" you ask him.

"That's *your* job," he replies. "But you sure haven't done it well so far."

You backspace over the three or four words you've written and start again. This time you get to the sixth or seventh word before your boss interrupts you again. "Don't they teach you people to spell anymore?" he says. "It's *i* before *e* except after *c*."

"Oh, that's right," you reply, and fix the error.

And so on. This bozo stands behind you as you write the entire story, sometimes correcting your grammar, sometimes criticizing your word choice, and sometimes fixing your punctuation.

Who could work under such conditions?

But that's what we all do to ourselves, at least some of the time. As one-stage writers (as shown in Figure 6-2), we wear both the writer's fedora and the editor's eyeshade at the same time. As we write a letter, memo, or report, our Internal Writer has to work very hard to coordinate the muscles that form the words. But at the same time that it's doing that, it also has to listen to our Internal Editor hassling it about every word and sentence.

And nobody hassles us like our Internal Editor does. It's had great teachers: our parents, all our teachers, all our bosses. In fact, our Internal Editor is precisely those parents, teachers, and bosses preserved intact in

Figure 6-2   One-stage writing.

our minds long after they've left our lives. As we write, that inner voice is always there, word by word, sentence by sentence, making us insecure about what we're saying and how we're saying it.

And as we write, our Internal Writer and Internal Editor are locked in a struggle for available time and resources. That struggle—as first one is in control and then the other—wastes time. In fact, a 2001 University of Michigan study found that workers waste 20 to 40 percent of their productivity by "task switching," readjusting mentally as they move from one kind of activity to another.

We may sometimes feel that the only way to stop that internal conflict is to do what Raymond has done in Figure 6-3.

A better solution, though, is to do what real writers and editors do. A good newspaper editor makes the best assignment he can and then gets out of the way. A good editor lets a writer be a writer, doing a writer's job without interference. Only when a draft has been written does the editor come back on the scene to review and revise.

Good writers and good editors work separately. By doing that, they each do their own job better. And the same is true of the Internal Writer and the Internal Editor. Accomplished writers keep their Internal Writer and Internal Editor separate. They wear one hat at a time.

Figure 6-3   Raymond puts a stop to his critical inner dialogue.

Writer Natalie Goldberg gave good advice: "It is important to separate the creator and the editor or internal censor. . . . If the editor is absolutely annoying . . . sit down whenever you need to and write what the editor is saying: give it full voice—'You are a jerk, who ever said you could write, I hate your work, you suck. I'm embarrassed, you have nothing valuable to say, and besides, you can't spell. . . .' Sound familiar?"

"The more clearly you know the editor," she continued, "the better you can ignore it. After a while, like the jabbering of an old drunk fool, it becomes just prattle in the background."

And Daphne Gray-Grant wrote in her great newsletter *Power Writing*, "Separate the writing and editing processes. When [effective writers] write, they write, not worrying about the quality of their work. Writer/director Cecil Castelluci says, 'The best flowers are fertilized by crap.' Remember this and give yourself permission to write a really crummy first draft. Editing is a job for later."

Now you know why the five-stage writing process works. So far in the course you've just had to take my word for its value. Now you've learned the psychology behind it.

When you have a writing job to do, wear one hat at a time. Before you let your Internal Writer go to work, demand that your Internal Editor make the most complete assignment possible. In other words, use your Internal Editor to go through the planning stage of the writing process following the steps covered so far in this course:

1. **Find the "we."** Identify the community to which you and your reader both belong. Consider the ways you and your reader are alike and different in the PACK dimensions: personality, attitude, circumstances, and knowledge.
2. **Make holes, not drills.** Establish the purpose of your writing. Are you writing conversation, correspondence, covenant, or conception? Are you writing to tell your reader about something, to ask your reader to do something, or both?
3. **Get your stuff together.** Gather the information that you want to include in the letter, memo, or report. Decide what goes in and what stays out.
4. **Get your ducks in a row.** Determine the order in which your reader should get your information. What should come first? second? last?

At this point, your Internal Editor will have an incredibly detailed assignment to give to your Internal Writer: "I want you to write for this reader, for this purpose, using these materials, in this order. And here are a lot of details about each." Don't you feel more confident about your work when your boss tells you more clearly what he or she wants? Well, by going through a good planning stage, that's what you can do for yourself.

When your Internal Editor has made a complete assignment, then get him or her out of the way so that your Internal Writer can draft without interference. This is easier said than done, of course. With practice, however, you can learn to turn off your Internal Editor while you produce the quick and dirty drafts recommended in Chapter 5. As the title of that chapter said, you can learn to give yourself permission to "Do It Wrong the First Time."

If the 10-minute nonstop writing exercise in Chapter 5 was hard for you, you can now see why. Your Internal Editor kept trying to horn in.

The break stage recommended in this chapter is your opportunity to change hats again. After a break, the Internal Editor can come back into the room and read the draft as if someone else wrote it—because, in a way, someone else did.

Obviously, this distinction somewhat oversimplifies the matter. At the planning and revising stages, your Internal Editor sometimes needs to call on your Internal Writer to make notes (at the planning stage) or to actually make the changes (at the revising stage). In general, though, you can learn to wear one hat at a time. As newsman Don Marquis once said, "I never think when I write; nobody can do two things at the same time and do them well."

Exercise

The following questions will test your understanding of this chapter. The final examination for this course will include similar questions.

1. At what stage of the writing process should you decide the order in which you will present your main points?
   a. Managing
   b. Planning
   c. Drafting
   d. Revising
2. At what stage of the writing process should you make sure a word is spelled correctly?
   a. Managing
   b. Planning
   c. Drafting
   d. Revising
3. At what stage of the writing process should you decide between two words with approximately the same meaning?
   a. Managing
   b. Planning

     c. Drafting

     d. Revising

4. At what stage of the writing process should you put sentences down on paper or on a computer screen?

     a. Managing

     b. Planning

     c. Drafting

     d. Revising

5. At what stage of the writing process should you determine the purpose of your writing?

     a. Managing

     b. Planning

     c. Drafting

     d. Revising

6. At what stage of the writing process should you allocate time for the other stages in the process?

     a. Managing

     b. Planning

     c. Drafting

     d. Revising

7. At what stage of the writing process should you get a general idea of how to start and end the piece of writing?

     a. Managing

     b. Planning

     c. Drafting

     d. Revising

8. At what stage of the writing process should you review a paragraph to see if it has enough transition words?

     a. Managing

     b. Planning

     c. Drafting

     d. Revising

9. At what stage of the writing process should you get an initial sense of your audience?
   a. Managing
   b. Planning
   c. Drafting
   d. Revising

10. At what stage of the writing process should you collect any information you need?
    a. Managing
    b. Planning
    c. Drafting
    d. Revising

MANAGE YOUR WRITING *TODAY*

On the very next writing job you have to do, begin with some writing management: Remind yourself that you're a writer, that writing can be managed, and that it's largely a matter of managing time. Set up blocks of time for planning, drafting, and revising—with more time allocated for planning and revising than for drafting.

- Then call in your Internal Editor to make the best possible "assignment" for this writing task. Begin by spending five minutes "finding the 'we.'" Take another five minutes to ask yourself, "What is the smallest community to which my audience and I both belong?" and "How are my audience and I alike and different in the four PACK dimensions: personality, attitude, circumstances, and knowledge?" Spend another five minutes to "make holes, not drills" by defining the purpose of the piece of writing. Take another five minutes or so to "get your stuff together," to gather information for the piece of writing. Then end the planning stage with five minutes of "getting your ducks in a row," organizing your information to best achieve your purpose for your reader(s).

- Now "do it wrong the first time." Bring in your Internal Writer to draft your document with as little interference as possible from your Internal Editor.
- Then take a break—for as long as you can but for at least five minutes. Use this time to gain some objectivity about your draft and to "change hats" from your Internal Writer's rumpled fedora to your Internal Editor's eyeshade.
- When you return from the break, try to trick yourself into thinking that someone else wrote the draft, and look at it as if you're seeing it for the first time. Then revise your document using all the tools you already have in your toolbox.

When you've finished, take a few minutes to evaluate how the process worked for you. Evaluate especially whether "taking a break and changing hats" resulted in a more effective piece of writing at the end.

7

SIGNAL YOUR TURNS

Manage Your Paragraphs

Entrepreneur and writer Peter Hay told a story about Sam Cherr, cofounder of the great advertising agency Young & Rubicam. According to the story, Cherr required all marketing plans to be written in considerable detail. A young employee once brought such a plan, in the 200-page range, to Cherr. After several days with no response, the employee went to Cherr's office and asked what he thought of the plan. Cherr replied, "Is this the best you can do?"

The employee admitted that he probably could do better, so he took back the plan. After extensive rewriting, he resubmitted the 200 pages. Again, he waited in vain and finally asked Cherr's opinion. Again, Cherr responded, "Is this the best you can do?"

Disappointed again, the employee confessed that yes, he probably could do better. After a weekend of rewriting, he again submitted the plan. When, several days later, he hadn't heard back from Cherr, he again asked him what he thought. For a third time, Cherr replied, "Is this the best you can do?"

This time, the young employee gulped and confessed, "Yes, Mr. Cherr, that's the best I can do."

"In that case," said Sam Cherr, "I'll read it."

The story tells the truth that good writing depends on good revising. To many would-be writers, this truth comes as a surprise. If we don't think of writing as a process that can be managed like any other business process, we may imagine that "good" writers produce good writing the first time and therefore don't have to revise. Writers may even have painful memories from grade school, when *rewrite* was a bad word, something we had to do when we didn't write well enough at first, something that kept us in from recess.

In fact, some research shows that good writers revise *more*, not less, than ordinary writers. Historian Paul Fussell once reported, "Crappy work I do twice, good work I do three times." American novelist John Dos Passos raised the bar even higher when he said, "I do a lot of revising. Certain chapters six or seven times." And an entrepreneur I once worked for—a master of direct-mail sales—once worked with me through more than a dozen versions of a high-stakes sales letter.

Matt Linderman, of the software development firm 37Signals, wrote, "Whether we're authoring software or prose, rewriting is the key. Rewriting is when you turn good into great. It's true for books, blog posts, marketing copy, interfaces, codes, etc. For all of them, we grind it out. We get something down, share it, get feedback, revise, and then do it over again. We get where we're going via lots of wrong turns. Sometimes we even throw everything away and start over from scratch. Yeah, that can be frustrating. But if you never throw anything away, you're holding on to your worst ideas."

Despite the difficulty of revision, many professional writers take great pleasure in revising their drafts. I'm one of them. I love the opportunities revision gives me. As playwright Neil Simon wrote, "In baseball, you only get three swings and you're out. In rewriting, you get almost as many swings as you want and you know, sooner or later, you'll hit the ball."

TOOLS FOR REVISION

With this chapter, as Figure 7-1 shows, we move into the revising stage of the writing process. Despite some of the quotations you've just read, revising doesn't have to take forever. In a typical one-hour writing job, revision really can be done effectively in 20 to 30 minutes.

To revise effectively, we need the proper tools. This chapter and the next four provide such tools. Before we get to them, however, we need to make three points about revision tools:

1. Revision tools are not drafting tools.
2. Revision tools are not rules.
3. You already have most of the revision tools you need.

Let's look closely at each of these three points. First, the tools you'll learn in this book are tools for revision, not tools for drafting. That's important. When you learn new tools for improving your writing, your Internal Editor inevitably will try to get you to use those tools at the drafting stage. With each new tool, your Internal Editor will have one more thing to hassle your Internal Writer about as you draft.

Figure 7-1   Signal your turns.

I read once about a "psych-out" technique to use if you're playing tennis against a tough opponent. After watching your opponent warm up, you say to him, "As I've been watching you, I've finally realized how to improve my backhand. It's the way you hold your thumb. How do you do that exactly?"

Unless your opponent is onto you, he probably will say, "Gee, I don't know. I've never thought about it."

"Well, think about it," you say. "I'd really appreciate any advice from you."

Then you start the match. If your opponent has fallen into your trap, he'll be thinking about his thumb, perhaps for the first time. He'll focus on that thumb—not on the ball, not on the net, not on the lines of the court. And that may give you the edge you need.

That's how your Internal Editor works. Like your tennis opponent, your inner editorial voice may well concentrate on the most recent thing it has paid attention to. So please, please, please remember that the powerful tools you'll learn in Chapters 7 through 11 are revising tools, not drafting tools.

Second, keep in mind the important difference between tools and rules. When we all first learned to write, we were taught a number of so-called rules for writing. Some of those "rules" really were rules, and this book will enforce them in Chapter 11 when we "finish" our writing. Other so-called rules, however, were just teaching devices—or even folklore—important only in limited cases or at certain stages in our development as writers. These include such "rules" as "Don't begin sentences with *and*," "Don't use *I* or *you* in your writing," and "Don't end sentences with prepositions."

Most of the lessons you'll learn in these five chapters are not rules but tools. Rules say, "Do this. Don't do that." Tools say, "If you want to achieve this, then maybe you'll want to do that." Rules control *you*; tools help you *take* control. Lynn Gaertner-Johnston, in her Business Writing blog, has reduced all writing rules to one: "The only rule is what works for readers." Thomas Edison took things a step further, saying, "Hell, there are no rules here. We're trying to accomplish something."

These next five chapters, then, are designed to show you how to take better control of your writing at the revising stage of your writing process. These chapters emphasize that you don't have to use the first words, sentences, or paragraphs that occur to you—those that come as you write your draft. Instead, you can take charge of those words, sentences, and paragraphs and make them work for you. Once again, you can *manage* your writing.

The third point is that you already have most of the tools you need to revise effectively. As the introduction to this book suggested, you've acquired these tools by all the reading you've done in your life. If, for some reason, you stop reading this book right now, you'll already have become a better reviser just by having learned to revise not *while* you draft but *after* you draft. The tools you already have will be even more useful to you as you use them at a separate revision stage.

The additional tools in these five chapters have been carefully selected both because they're especially effective and because most of the writers I work with have not learned them before. Like most adult writers, you already have a pretty good basic tool kit—comparable to a hammer, a saw, screwdrivers, and pliers. I simply want to add to it by giving you, say, a socket wrench set and a power drill.

TURN SIGNALS

The late Malcolm Forbes said it best: "People who read business letters are as human as thee and me. Reading a letter shouldn't be a chore."

That's our job as writers—making the act of reading as easy as possible so that our readers can give all their attention to what we are saying. At the revising stage of our writing process, we need to make sure that our writing "flows," moving the reader smoothly from one sentence to the next.

Read the following paragraph. I think you'll agree that it doesn't flow. The sentences seem "choppy," with awkward changes of direction. The writer seems unsure about where she is going. The paragraph, in fact, isn't really a paragraph at all, just a collection of disconnected sentences. Reading it is, in Forbes's words, a chore.

> The next sample, Formula D-7, is an excellent adhesive. It was the strongest of any tested. It was one of the most water-resistant. It has several disadvantages. Its cost is fairly high. Its viscosity would perhaps require new application equipment. Its viscosity would perhaps require modifications in existing equipment. Its storage-temperature requirements are rather strict. In my judgment, these disadvantages are outweighed by its overall quality. I recommend that Formula D-7 be used for the project.

One important way to improve the readability of such writing—to make it less of a chore for your reader—is by using "turn signals," words or phrases that show the relationship of each sentence with a previous one.

Pretend that you and I work together and that our work team has planned a picnic on a Saturday morning. We're going to bring our families and meet in the company parking lot. Then I'm going to lead the convoy of cars out to a great picnic spot I know in the country.

It will really help you if I use turn signals. Without turn signals, you wouldn't be prepared for the turns I make. You might, in fact, become as exasperated as Jason in Figure 7-2. With turn signals, I'll be much easier to follow.

Figure 7-2   Jason brings a note of sarcasm to his driver critiques.

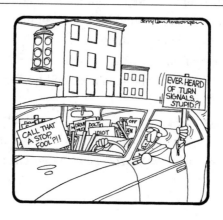

For exactly the same reason, the written "turn signals" we'll be talking about in this chapter make it easier for the reader to follow the writer through a memo, letter, or report. (Note that we already use the word *follow* when we talk about reading a piece of writing.)

To signal your turns in a piece of writing, you need to understand something about the relationships that sentences can have with each other. One authority on writing, Ross Winterowd, listed six kinds of relationships that can exist between sentences. These six relationships are listed in Figure 7-3. Each of these relationships has its own turn signals.

The first relationship can be signaled by the word *and*. Two sentences have an *and* relationship when the second sentence simply adds more information of the same kind. Therefore, an *and* relationship is like a plus sign in mathematics. Besides the word *and*, this relationship can be signaled with other words and phrases such as the following:

- also
- too
- moreover
- furthermore
- in addition
- next
- second
- third

Figure 7-3   Relationships between sentences.

And relationships can also be signaled by numbers or bullets in a list—like the list you just read. Such lists are extremely helpful to readers. One study of Web-based writing found that the use of headings and bullets increases usability by 47 percent.

Here's that sample paragraph again, this time with its sentences numbered so that we can refer to them more easily:

(1) The next sample, Formula D-7, is an excellent adhesive. (2) It was the strongest of any tested. (3) It was one of the most water-resistant. (4) It has several disadvantages. (5) Its cost is fairly high. (6) Its viscosity would perhaps require new application equipment. (7) Its viscosity would perhaps require modifications in existing equipment. (8) Its storage-temperature requirements are rather strict. (9) In my judgment, these disadvantages are outweighed by its overall quality. (10) I recommend that Formula D-7 be used for the project.

In this paragraph, the second and third sentences have an *and* relationship. The advantage cited in sentence 3 is meant to be *added*, in our reader's mind, to the advantage cited in sentence 2:

It was the strongest of any tested. It was one of the most water-resistant.

To signal this relationship to our reader, we can add the word *and* after the second sentence; then (as a bonus) we can eliminate the repeated words *It was* and combine the two sentences:

It was the strongest of any tested and one of the most water-resistant.

The next possible relationship is usually signaled by the word *or*. Two sentences have an *or* relationship when they present alternatives. Besides the word *or*, this relationship can be signaled with the words *alternatively* and *otherwise*.

Sentences 6 and 7, the two "viscosity" sentences, have an *or* relationship expressing alternative ways of solving a problem:

Its viscosity would perhaps require new application equipment. Its viscosity would perhaps require modifications in existing equipment.

We can make things easier for our reader by adding the word *or* between the sentences and by deleting the words *Its viscosity would perhaps require* the second time they are used:

Its viscosity would perhaps require new application equipment or modifications in existing equipment.

Once we have combined these two "viscosity" sentences, we now have a series of three sentences—the new combined sentence and sentences 5 and 8—about disadvantages of the adhesive. These sentences all have an *and* relationship, so we can make them into a series using the word *and*:

Its cost is fairly high, its viscosity would perhaps require new application equipment or modifications in existing equipment, and its storage-temperature requirements are rather strict.

Although this is a fairly long sentence, it's easier to read than the three disconnected sentences we had before. (Of course, we could make the three disadvantages into a bulleted list as another way of signaling their *and* relationship. In this particular paragraph, however, we may not want to call attention to the disadvantages in this way.)

The third relationship between sentences can be signaled by the word *but*. Two sentences have a *but* relationship when the second sentence contradicts, partially contradicts, or qualifies the first. Besides the word *but*, this relationship can be signaled with such words and phrases as the following:

- however
- nevertheless

- nonetheless
- on the other hand

One *but* relationship occurs before sentence 4:

> It has several disadvantages.

This sentence contradicts, or at least qualifies, the previous sentences, which were about advantages. So we can help our reader by adding a *but* turn signal to this sentence. For example, we could say, "It nevertheless has several disadvantages."

Similarly, sentence 9, the sentence beginning, "In my judgment," has a *but* relationship with the preceding sentences. Those preceding sentences were about disadvantages, but now we're about to make a positive judgment. For variety, we might add the word *However* at the beginning of this sentence to signal the turn:

> However, in my judgment, these disadvantages are outweighed by its overall quality.

The fourth and fifth possible relationships are really the same relationship seen from two different sides. Two sentences have a *so* relationship when the second expresses the result, conclusion, or effect of the first sentence. Besides the word *so*, this relationship can be signaled with such words and phrases as the following:

- therefore
- thus
- for this reason

The *because* relationship is the opposite of the *so* relationship: two sentences have a *because* relationship when the second gives the cause or reason for the first. Besides the word *because*, this relationship can be signaled with such words as *since* and *for*.

In the sample paragraph, sentences 9 and 10 have a *so* relationship. We might signal this relationship by adding the word *therefore* to the last sentence at any of several points near the beginning of that sentence.

However, in my judgment, these disadvantages are outweighed by its overall quality. I therefore recommend that Formula D-7 be used for the project.

The last relationship is often signaled with a punctuation mark, the *colon*. Two sentences have a *colon* relationship when the second sentence gives specifics for the generalization made in the first sentence. Beside a colon, this relationship can be signaled with such words and phrases as the following:

- specifically
- for example
- to illustrate

Sentence 1 of the sample paragraph has a *colon* relationship with the combined sentence that follows it. The first sentence says that the adhesive is excellent; the next sentences give the specific ways it is excellent. So we can signal where we are going by adding a colon after that first sentence:

The next sample, Formula D-7, is an excellent adhesive: it was the strongest of any tested and one of the most water-resistant.

In the same way, the sentence reporting that the adhesive has several disadvantages has a *colon* relationship with the following series. Therefore, we can put a colon after that sentence as well:

It nevertheless has several disadvantages: its cost is fairly high, its viscosity would perhaps require new application equipment or modifications in existing equipment, and its storage-temperature requirements are rather strict.

The following paragraph shows the result of adding all these turn signals—and, as a by-product, deleting some repeated words. I hope you agree that it's much improved. This particular information could be presented in other ways—in a table, for example. However, whenever you're writing sentences, you can use turn signals to make your writing much easier to read:

> The next sample, Formula D-7, is an excellent adhesive: it was the strongest of any tested and one of the most water-resistant. It nevertheless has several disadvantages: its cost is fairly high, its viscosity would perhaps require new application equipment or modifications in existing equipment, and its storage-temperature requirements are rather strict. However, in my judgment, these disadvantages are outweighed by its overall quality. I therefore recommend that Formula D-7 be used for the project.

One final note: if you go back now and read the original paragraph, you may find that it looks better to you than it did at first. This is so because you now know where it's going. You don't need as many turn signals.

That's the position you're always in when you read your own drafts. Because you know where you're going, you may not feel a need for turn signals. But turn signals aren't for *you*. They're for the person *following* you.

Bill Jensen, in his book *Simplicity*, expressed this issue well: "When people are *in need of* communication, they want others to take the time to listen, and then to take the time to create meaning, clarity, and connections between ideas. But when they have to *do the communicating*, saving time becomes a priority. . . . When it comes to communication, business is facing major discipline and accountability problems. It's like the line about change: Taking the time to create clarity is important—as long as it's the other guy who has to do it."

Don't fall into this trap. Use turn signals even more than you think you need to. If you do, reading your memos, letters, and reports won't be a chore for your readers.

Exercises

Exercise A

The following questions will test your understanding of this chapter. The final examination for this course will include similar questions.

1. Which of the following shows the most effective use of turn signals?
    a. Capacity is more than 2.5 million barrels per day. Current production is much lower.
    b. Capacity is more than 2.5 million barrels per day, but current production is much lower.
    c. Capacity is more than 2.5 million barrels per day, and current production is much lower.
    d. Capacity is more than 2.5 million barrels per day, because current production is much lower.

2. Which of the following shows the most effective use of turn signals?
    a. The emirate produces liquefied natural gas. The emirate produces natural gas liquids.
    b. The emirate produces liquefied natural gas. However, the emirate produces natural gas liquids.
    c. The emirate produces liquefied natural gas and natural gas liquids.
    d. The emirate produces liquefied natural gas, but the emirate produces natural gas liquids.

3. Which of the following shows the most effective use of turn signals?
    a. NGL is produced in two plants. One is on Das Island. One is at Ruwais.
    b. NGL is produced in two plants. One is on Das Island, but one is at Ruwais.
    c. NGL is produced in two plants. Therefore, one is on Das Island. One is at Ruwais.
    d. NGL is produced in two plants: One is on Das Island and the other at Ruwais.

4. Which of the following shows the most effective use of turn signals?
    a. Some emirates have a corporate tax law, but it is applied only to foreign oil companies and foreign banks operating in those emirates.
    b. Some emirates have a corporate tax law. Therefore, it is applied only to foreign oil companies and foreign banks operating in those emirates.

c. Some emirates have a corporate tax law. And it is applied only to foreign oil companies and foreign banks operating in those emirates.

d. Some emirates have a corporate tax law, so it is applied only to foreign oil companies and foreign banks operating in those emirates.

5. **Which of the following shows the most effective use of turn signals?**
   a. The meeting was very beneficial, but new subjects were discussed.
   b. The meeting was very beneficial, so new subjects were discussed.
   c. The meeting was very beneficial because new subjects were discussed.
   d. The meeting was very beneficial; however, new subjects were discussed.

6. **Which of the following shows the most effective use of turn signals?**
   a. The subcommittee report did not arrive in time. It had to be mailed to participants later.
   b. The subcommittee report did not arrive in time, but it had to be mailed to participants later.
   c. The subcommittee report did not arrive in time, and it had to be mailed to participants later.
   d. The subcommittee report did not arrive in time, so it had to be mailed to participants later.

7. **Which of the following shows the most effective use of turn signals?**
   a. The report will cover traditional uses of LPG. It will cover use of LPG as an alternative transport fuel.
   b. The report will cover both traditional uses of LPG and its use as an alternative transport fuel.
   c. The report will cover traditional uses of LPG. However, it will cover uses of LPG as an alternative transport fuel.
   d. The report will cover traditional uses of LPG, but it will cover its uses as an alternative transport fuel.

8. **Which of the following shows the most effective use of turn signals?**
   a. The course will examine global supply and demand balances. The course will examine regional supply and demand balances.
   b. The course will examine global supply and demand balances, but it will examine regional supply and demand balances.

     c. The course will examine global supply and demand balances. The course also will examine regional supply and demand balances.

     d. The course will examine global and regional supply and demand balances.

9. Which of the following shows the most effective use of turn signals?

     a. The February meeting was canceled. Many participants would be unable to attend.

     b. The February meeting was canceled, and many participants would be unable to attend.

     c. The February meeting was canceled, but many participants would be unable to attend.

     d. The February meeting was canceled because many participants would be unable to attend.

10. Which of the following shows the most effective use of turn signals?

     a. The writing process has five stages. They are managing, planning, drafting, breaking, and revising.

     b. The writing process has five stages: managing, planning, drafting, breaking, and revising.

     c. The writing process has five stages. But they are managing, planning, drafting, breaking, and revising.

     d. The writing process has five stages. Therefore, they are managing, planning, drafting, breaking, and revising.

Exercise B

Revise the following memo, signaling turns more effectively and making any other changes that will improve it.

In the past, procedures for repair and calibration of test equipment have been unsatisfactory. Too much time has been spent taking instruments to Instrument Services. Employees have spent too much time picking equipment up from Instrument Services. Misplacement of some equipment has occurred.

On November 10 a new procedure will go into effect. "Drop zones" have been created for the pickup of test equipment. If you have instruments in need of calibration, take them to the appropriate drop zone in your building. Drop zones will be used for repair of instruments. Managers may consult the attached list for drop zone locations. Pickup will occur twice weekly. It will occur on Mondays and Thursdays.

Managers will be responsible for getting their equipment to the drop zone. They may send representatives to do it. Returns will be made by Instrument Services personnel. To ensure that instruments are returned to the correct manager, have the correct department and building number marked on each instrument before taking it to the drop zone.

Inquiries about whether an instrument has been repaired or calibrated should be directed to Instrument Services. Do not call the drop zone coordinator to find out if a piece of equipment is ready. Managers should call Instrument Services if they have any questions on the drop zone system.

MANAGE YOUR WRITING *TODAY*

On the very next writing job you have to do, begin with some writing management: Remind yourself that you're a writer, that writing can be managed, and that it's largely a matter of managing time. Set up blocks of time for planning, drafting, and revising—with more time allocated for planning and revising than for drafting.

- Then call in your Internal Editor to make the best possible "assignment" for this writing task. Begin by spending five minutes "finding the 'we.'" Take another five minutes to ask yourself, "What is the smallest community to which my audience and I both belong?" and "How are my audience and I alike and different in the four PACK dimensions: personality, attitude, circumstances, and knowledge?" Spend another five minutes to "make holes, not drills" by defining the purpose of the piece of writing. Take another five minutes or so to "get your stuff together," to gather information for the piece of writing. Then end the planning stage with five minutes of "getting your ducks in a row," organizing your information to best achieve your purpose for your reader(s).

- Next "do it wrong the first time." Bring in your Internal Writer to draft your document, with as little interference as possible from your Internal Editor.
- Then take a break—for as long as you can, but for at least five minutes. Use this time to gain some objectivity about your draft and to "change hats" from your Internal Writer's rumpled fedora to your Internal Editor's eyeshade.
- When you return from the break, try to trick yourself into thinking that someone else wrote the draft, and look at it as if you're seeing it for the first time. Then revise your document using all the tools you already have in your toolbox. However, pay special attention to "signaling your turns," guiding your reader from sentence to sentence.

When you've finished, take a few minutes to evaluate how the process worked for you. Evaluate especially whether using turn signals resulted in a more effective piece of writing at the end.

8

SAY WHAT YOU MEAN

Manage Your Subjects and Verbs

Daniel Defoe, author of *Robinson Crusoe*, also wrote one of the first business how-to books in English, *The Complete English Tradesman*, published in 1745. In that book, Defoe wrote, "A tradesman's letters should be plain, concise, and to the purpose. . . . He that affects a rumbling and bombast style and fills his letter with compliments and flourishes makes a very ridiculous figure in trade."

After more than 250 years, Defoe's advice stills holds up. Like Connie in Figure 8-1, effective business writing gets to the point and says what it means. Specifically, it matches the structure of each sentence (what the sentence *says*) with the content of that sentence (what the sentence *means*).

As Figure 8-2 shows, we're now at the second step in the revising stage of the writing process. At this step we focus on managing sentence structure, especially the subjects and verbs of our sentences.

This is the first chapter that uses grammatical terms. But please don't worry if your knowledge of formal grammar is somewhat fuzzy.

Figure 8-1   Connie always lets Glen know when she's happy.

By the end of this chapter you'll have learned, through examples, all you need to know about verbs and subjects.

As you work your way through this chapter, remember the three points made at the beginning of Chapter 7:

1. Revision tools are not drafting tools.
2. Revision tools are not rules.
3. You already have most of the revision tools you need.

Figure 8-2   Say what you mean.

Remember especially the first point. When you're drafting—"doing it wrong the first time"—you should not worry about grammar.

So let's get to it. Arthur Levitt, former chairman of the U.S. Securities and Exchange Commission, once said that in bad business writing, "the prose trips off the tongue like peanut butter." Let's learn how to change that.

HIDDEN SUBJECTS

At this step in the revising stage, your main job is to check that most of your grammatical subjects and verbs are the *real* subjects and verbs of your sentences.

Let's begin with subjects. Look at the following sentence:

It is difficult to control costs.

The grammatical subject is *it*, but that's hardly the *real* subject, the noun or pronoun the sentence is about. The reader subconsciously tries to find meaning in that subject and comes up empty-handed.

The *real* subject of the sentence is *costs* or, perhaps, *control*, both "hidden" later in the sentence. The sentence can be improved by making the hidden, real subject also the grammatical subject. So consider revising the sentence to one of the following:

Costs are difficult to control.

or

Controlling costs is difficult.

When the reader reads the subject of either of these sentences, he or she knows what the sentence is about. The sentence says what it means.

One common place to find hidden subjects is in sentences beginning with *There*:

> There needs to be more tribute paid to these unselfish workers.

The real subject of this sentence is not *There* but *tribute* or perhaps even *workers*. Depending on which of these nouns you want to emphasize, you could improve the sentence in either of two ways:

> More tribute should be paid to these unselfish workers.

or

> These unselfish workers deserve more tribute.

HIDDEN VERBS

Even more common than hidden subjects are hidden verbs. English has a tendency—no, English *tends*—to "nominalize"—to make verbs into nouns. *Tend*, for example, is a verb, but it is often changed into the noun *tendency*. Once you have made that change, you don't have a verb in your sentence anymore, so you insert a "filler" verb such as *has, gives*, or *makes*:

> He *tends* to be late.
> He *has* a *tendency* to be late.

Ruth Walker, writing in *The Christian Science Monitor*, decried this phenomenon: "Look what's happening to verbs—the 'muscles' of language. They're being crowded out by more sedate linking-verb constructions. . . . 'He lost his job' often loses out to 'He became unemployed.' Instead of 'Ace Insurance Agency serves the maritime industry,' we often get, 'Ace is a provider of insurance services to the maritime industry.'"

With this in mind, look at this sentence:

> The committee reached an agreement on the project.

The verb is *reached*, but this is not the *real* verb, the action that the committee performed. The committee didn't *reach*; it *agreed*. *Reached* is a filler verb; the real verb, *agree*, has been changed into the noun *agreement*. So consider revising the sentence to "The committee agreed on the project."

Here's a sentence from a report I once edited:

The consumer must make intelligent choices when buying tires.

The verb in this sentence is *make*. But is the consumer really making something? No. What the sentence *means* is that the consumer must *choose*. So we can improve this sentence by making it say what it means:

The consumer must choose intelligently when buying tires.

Alternatively, since the word *consumer* implies buying, we might revise the sentence even further:

The consumer must choose tires intelligently.

Here's another:

Ellen made a recommendation that we conduct a survey of employee morale.

This sentence has two clauses, each with its own verb: *made* and *conduct*. Both are empty filler verbs. In each clause the real action has been hidden in a noun: *recommendation* and *survey*. The sentence will be stronger if we turn those hidden verbs into real verbs:

Ellen recommended that we survey employee morale.

Writer and consultant Lee Wood gave me a particularly good (bad?) example of a hidden verb. She once revised the following sentence:

Membership will be twice as much next year.

into

Membership will double next year.

Don't you agree that the revised sentence is much stronger with the verb *double* replacing the verb *be*?

HIDDEN SUBJECTS *AND* VERBS

Pay special attention to sentences beginning with *It is*, *There is*, and *There are*. Such sentences often have neither the *real* subject nor the *real* verb in the subject and verb positions:

1. It is not until Wednesday that the parts will arrive.
2. There is a wide range of costs.
3. There are three reasons why you should expand the product line.

The grammatical subjects and verbs of all three sentences are absolutely empty.

In sentence 1, the real subject is *parts*, and the real verb is *arrive*. Consider revising it to, "The parts will arrive Wednesday" or "The parts will not arrive until Wednesday" (depending on whether you're the supplier, promising, or the buyer, complaining).

In business writing, the *It is* combination is so common that humorist Dave Barry made fun of it in his book *Claw Your Way to the Top*: "State that something is your understanding. This statement should be firm, vaguely disapproving, and virtually impossible to understand. A good standard one is: 'It is my understanding that this was to be ascertained in advance of any further action, pending review.'"

In sentence 2, the real subject is *costs*, and the real verb is *range*. Therefore, revise it to "Costs range widely."

Novelist Philip Roth probably was referring to just this kind of revision when he wrote, "I turn sentences around. That's my life. I write a sentence and then I turn it around. Then I look at it and I turn it around again."

Often, as in sentence 3, you'll have a choice about which noun or pronoun in the sentence should be made the subject. If you want to emphasize the three reasons, make *reasons* the subject:

Three reasons why you should expand the product line are . . .

If you want to emphasize the reader, make *you* the subject:

You should expand the product line for three reasons.

If you want to emphasize the product line, make *line* the subject:

The product line should be expanded for three reasons.

Therefore, consider revising sentences such as "It is helpful to check subjects and verbs" to "Checking subjects and verbs helps." You'll be saying what you mean, and you'll be a more effective manager of your writing.

ACTIVE OR PASSIVE

As for verbs themselves, they generally are more readable and effective when they are active, not passive. Consider these sentences:

The book was ordered by us last week.
We ordered the book last week.

In the first sentence, the verb is passive: The subject (*book*) "receives" the action of the verb (*was ordered*). The second sentence is much more effective: The subject (*we*) is "doing" the acting, so the verb (*ordered*) is active.

To locate passive verbs, look for an action verb in its past participle form (usually ending in *-ed*), preceded by a form of the verb *to be* (*is, are, was, were, be, am,* or *been*). In most such cases, the person or thing doing the acting comes later in the sentence or is left out entirely. See whether you can improve the sentence by moving that word (or words) earlier, making it the subject of the sentence, and changing the verb into an active one.

At times, however, you will want to use a passive verb instead of an active one. For example, if the *real* subject of your sentence receives the action of the verb, then a passive verb may be more effective. In technical and scientific writing in particular, the real subject is often the passive recipient of procedures and tests:

The sample was heated to 500ºC and subjected to Test B. The following changes were observed.

To put these sentences into active form ("I heated the sample. . . . I observed the following changes") would put far too much emphasis on the writer. So like other principles of revision you've learned in this course, changing verbs to their active form is a tool, not a rule. Journalist William Safire, in his book *Fumblerules*, made fun of people who preach that active verbs are always better. "The passive voice," he writes passively, "should never be used."

The tool of changing passive verbs to active verbs is a useful safeguard against the unthinking overuse of passive verbs, but it should not be applied when there is good reason to use the passive voice.

One final note about passive verbs: They can be used to avoid taking responsibility. Notice the difference between "I made mistakes" and "Mistakes were made." Every politician prefers the latter, and every voter should see through it.

MODIFIERS

Pulitzer Prize winner J. Anthony Lukas once said, "If the noun is good and the verb is strong, you almost never need an adjective." Still, we can't do completely without modifiers—adjectives and adverbs.

To revise modifiers, it helps to understand something about how people read. Readers, as they move through a sentence, continually move words and phrases into memory. But memory is of two kinds, and knowing this can help you as you revise your sentences.

The two kinds of memory, short term and long term, are like the short- and long-term parking lots at many airports. Short-term parking lots are usually close to the terminal and thus more convenient, but they are also smaller and more expensive. Long-term parking lots are larger and cheaper but more remote.

Short-term memory, too, is "closer" to the immediate perception of words on a page. As words are read, they are stored in short-term memory *as words*. But space in short-term memory is limited; some psychologists estimate its capacity at five to nine "items." Thus, as soon as individual words can be grouped together into meaningful units, they are moved "farther back" into long-term memory. Here they are stored not as words but as meanings. As an example, you almost certainly cannot remember now the exact wording of my paragraph comparing memory with parking lots. But you do remember (I hope) the paragraph's meaning.

One goal, then, of the revising stage should be to let the reader, as often as possible, combine words into larger meanings in order to transfer them into long-term memory. If this combining is delayed too long, the short-term memory becomes overloaded and empties, and the reader must backtrack in the sentence to figure out what it's about.

And this brings us back to subjects and verbs. If too many modifiers separate the subject and verb, the short-term memory gets overloaded and reading becomes difficult. Consider this sentence:

> A new federal regulation regarding the sale of snack foods in competition with federally subsidized meal programs in schools is in effect this fall.

Here, the subject, *regulation*, must be held in suspension while a 15-word modifier goes by before the verb, *is*, comes along. The readability of this sentence can be improved greatly if the long modifier is postponed until after the verb. This keeps the subject and verb close enough together that they can easily be combined and moved into long-term memory:

> A new federal regulation is in effect this fall, a regulation regarding the sale of snack foods in competition with federally subsidized meal programs in schools.

Notice that the word *regulation* has been repeated to keep it close to the phrase that modifies it.

Here's another example from the same report:

> In addition, the judge who ruled to uphold the regulation in two suits brought against the department said that the USDA could not exempt fortified foods from any of the restricted categories of food.

This sentence is more readable if revised like this:

> In addition, in two suits brought against the department, the judge upholding the regulation said the USDA could not exempt fortified foods from any of the restricted categories of food.

The best place for modifiers is usually after the subject and verb. Extensive use of final modifiers, especially ones separated from the subject and verb by punctuation, is a relatively recent development in the English language but an extraordinarily valuable one. Francis Christensen, who first called this development to wide attention, labeled sentences with separated final modifiers as "cumulative sentences." Here's an example:

> The engineers concentrated their efforts on total efficiency, the highest possible ratio between energy-out and energy-in, not just on one or two isolated areas.

Such cumulative sentences have a powerful advantage for the reader: They require almost no suspension of words in short-term memory, almost no backtracking to pick up modifiers. The subject and verb come early ("The engineers concentrated"), and thus they can be combined into a single meaning and moved immediately into long-term memory. The subsequent modifiers refer to things that have been named already, and so they, too, can be moved quickly to long-term memory to join the things they modify. One key to creating effective, readable sentences is to stop thinking of sentences existing in space—on paper or on screen—and start thinking of your sentences as existing in time, as a reader processes them.

A fringe benefit of cumulative sentences is that they are remarkably easy to write. As you begin revising your sentences into cumulative form, you'll find that more cumulative sentences will start coming out on their own at the drafting stage. When you write a cumulative sentence, you don't need to invent the entire sentence and hold it in your mind before you begin to write it. Instead, you can write your subject and verb; drop in a colon, dash, or comma; and then provide the details. That's just what the writer of this sentence did:

> I suggest a new advertising campaign, aimed not at our traditional teenage market but at the growing number of twenty- to-thirty-year-olds, a campaign emphasizing not glamour but economy.

Exercises

Exercise A

The following questions will test your understanding of this chapter. The final examination for this course will include similar questions.

1. Which of the following sentences manages subjects and verbs most effectively?
   a. It seems probable that we will be unable to participate.
   b. We probably can't participate.

     c.   Our participation will not be probable.

     d.   There is a low probability that we will be able to participate.

2. **Which of the following sentences manages subjects and verbs most effectively?**

     a.   We need to understand the strategy better.

     b.   We have a need to gain a better understanding of the strategy.

     c.   We need to gain a better understanding of the strategy.

     d.   We have a need to understand the strategy better.

3. **Which of the following sentences manages subjects and verbs most effectively?**

     a.   I would like you to determine how such a process would be of benefit to us.

     b.   Please make a determination of how such a process would be of benefit to us.

     c.   Please determine how such a process would benefit us.

     d.   I would like you to make a determination of how such a process would benefit us.

4. **Which of the following sentences manages subjects and verbs most effectively?**

     a.   It is difficult to control total expenses.

     b.   There is a difficulty in the control of total expenses.

     c.   Total expenses are difficult to control.

     d.   It is the case that total expenses are difficult to control.

5. **Which of the following sentences manages subjects and verbs most effectively?**

     a.   It is my opinion that market segmentation issues are clear.

     b.   It is my opinion that there is clarity in market segmentation issues.

     c.   I believe that there is clarity in market segmentation issues.

     d.   I believe that market segmentation issues are clear.

6. **Which of the following sentences manages subjects and verbs most effectively?**

     a.   Currently, there is no defined career development process within headquarters.

     b.   Currently, headquarters has no defined career development process.

     c.   There is currently no defined career development process within headquarters.

     d.   At the current time, there is no defined career development process within headquarters.

7. Which of the following sentences manages subjects and verbs most effectively?
   a. It is my hope that you will submit a proposal.
   b. I hope that you will submit a proposal.
   c. Your submission of a proposal is my hope.
   d. I hope that you will make a proposal submission.

8. Which of the following sentences manages subjects and verbs most effectively?
   a. The course will examine global supply and demand balances.
   b. The course will make an examination of global supply and demand balances.
   c. An examination of global supply and demand balances will be made by the course.
   d. There will be in the course an examination of global supply and demand balances.

9. Which of the following sentences manages subjects and verbs most effectively?
   a. The April meeting was canceled by action of the director.
   b. The cancellation of the April meeting was made by the director.
   c. The director declared the April meeting canceled.
   d. The director canceled the April meeting.

10. Which of the following sentences manages subjects and verbs most effectively?
   a. The writing process has five stages.
   b. There are five stages in the writing process.
   c. It is the case that the writing process has five stages.
   d. It is the case that there are five stages in the writing process.

Exercise B

Revise the following memo, managing subjects and verbs more effectively and making any other changes that will improve it.

There have been a number of public statements made by several of you about our company in recent weeks. These statements are believed by me to be harmful to the public image of the C&E Company.

I made a referral of this matter to the Board of Directors, who held a discussion of it at some length. The Board made the decision that in the future all public statements about our company must be given advance clearance by this office. There are forms available for this purpose.

Your cooperation in this matter will be appreciated.

MANAGE YOUR WRITING *TODAY*

On the very next writing job you have to do, begin with some writing management: Remind yourself that you're a writer, that writing can be managed, and that it's largely a matter of managing time. Set up blocks of time for planning, drafting, and revising—with more time allocated for planning and revising than for drafting.

- Then call in your Internal Editor to make the best possible "assignment" for this writing task. Begin by spending five minutes "finding the 'we.'" Take another five minutes to ask yourself, "What is the smallest community to which my audience and I both belong?" and "How are my audience and I alike and different in the four PACK dimensions: personality, attitude, circumstances, and knowledge?" Spend another five minutes to "make holes, not drills" by defining the purpose of the piece of writing. Take another five minutes or so to "get your stuff together," to gather information for the piece of writing. Then end the planning stage with five minutes of "getting your ducks in a row," organizing your information to best achieve your purpose for your reader(s).
- Next "do it wrong the first time." Bring in your Internal Writer to draft your document, with as little interference as possible from your Internal Editor.
- Then take a break—for as long as you can, but for at least five minutes. Use this time to gain some objectivity about your draft and to "change hats" from your Internal Writer's rumpled fedora to your Internal Editor's eyeshade. When you return from the break, try to

trick yourself into thinking that someone else wrote the draft, and look at it as if you're seeing it for the first time.

- Then revise your document using all the tools you already have in your toolbox. However, pay special attention to "signaling your turns," guiding your reader from sentence to sentence, and to "saying what you mean" by managing your subjects and verbs.

When you've finished, take a few minutes to evaluate how the process worked for you. Evaluate especially whether "saying what you mean" resulted in a more effective piece of writing at the end.

9

PAY BY THE WORD

Manage Your Sentence Economy

orman R. Augustine, president and CEO of Martin Marietta, once calculated the relationship between thickness and dollar amount of government contract proposals. After reporting the result, he wrote, "If all the proposals conforming to this standard were piled on top of each other at the bottom of the Grand Canyon, it would probably be a good idea."

Most readers of government and business writing agree that much of it is too long. But who's to blame? The comic strip character Pogo had the answer: "We have met the enemy, and he is us." Simply put, most writers in business and government use more words than they need to.

Some trainers and textbooks talk about "conciseness" or "brevity." I prefer the word *economy*, for two reasons. First, the words *conciseness* and *brevity* suggest that the best sentences are the shortest. But that's not always true. Remember when we added turn signals to a very "choppy" paragraph in Chapter 7? We actually made some sentences longer but also more effective. The word *economy*, however, suggests *value*. The most economical car is not necessarily the smallest or cheapest. It's the one that gives you the most of what you need at the lowest cost. Similarly, some sentences have to be relatively long to say what they mean. Economical sentences just don't use more words than they need.

The second reason I like the word *economy* is that it suggests money—euros, pounds, and dollars. Business is about money. As someone once said, in the game of business, money is how we keep score.

You see, many of us write as if we were getting paid by the word. This habit may come from our childhood and adolescence, when we were assigned to write school papers with specific word counts: the famous 500-word theme, for example. In my early days as a teacher—before I knew better—I remember getting handwritten 500-word themes with a running word count in the margin—397, 440, 472, 489, 495—as the writer closed in on the magic number.

In fact, relatively few writers, and probably no business writers, get paid by the word. Instead, we *pay* by the word. Economic writing is writing that literally saves us money, in both the short and the long term.

In the short term, writing costs money to produce, both in materials and in time. Norman Augustine, again, calculated that "a single copy of a winning proposal for a modern aircraft requires a document embodying a preparation cost per pound . . . about 400 times the cost per pound of the aircraft itself." And Ed Reilly, president and chief executive of the American Management Association, told the *New York Times*, "Companies go to great lengths to set up lists of authorized approvals, meaning who can approve what size of purchase. But you will find that people who are not authorized to spend $100 on their own are authorized to send e-mails to people and waste hundreds of thousands of dollars' worth of company time."

What also adds up is the cost of failures to communicate, even to innovate, caused by unnecessarily wordy writing. Many companies are learning the value of sentence economy. A vice president at 3M, legendary for its innovation, told Tom Peters, "We consider a coherent sentence to be an acceptable first draft for a new-product plan."

But even more important, perhaps, is writing's long-term cost in terms of our readers' attention and goodwill. As Quentin E. Wood, CEO of Quaker State, once said, "When you say less, and say it more clearly, people remember more of it—and longer." This is so because, in fact, each unnecessary word costs us some of the attention and goodwill of each of our readers. As Matt Stibbe wrote on his blog Bad Language, "You have no right to your readers' time."

Consider this analogy. Suppose that next Monday you arrive at your office and find an envelope from me. Inside is a $10 bill. Tuesday and Wednesday you find the same. By Thursday, you're thinking about me during your commute, looking forward with pleasure to opening my envelope. By the time the last envelope comes on Friday, you're feeling very good about Ken Davis and the $50 I've sent you.

Now suppose, instead, that Monday's envelope holds a dollar. On Tuesday there's a quarter, and on Wednesday, 75 cents. You're intrigued, then disappointed, when Thursday's envelope, sealed with strapping tape, holds only a nickel. The letters keep coming, on into the next week and the weeks after, some with as much as a couple of dollars but most with small change. My envelopes become less and less important to you. Even if after several months you've received the same $50, you don't feel nearly as good about me. You've simply had to work too hard for the money.

This is how reading is. Reading a word is like opening an envelope: It requires a small but measurable amount of work. If each envelope or word contains something of value, we continue with anticipation. If most envelopes or words do not, we become bored and maybe give up. Thus, when you use 100 words instead of 200 to say something, you not only save money, but also have a much better chance of keeping your reader's attention and goodwill. In the early nineteenth century, British author C. C. Colton knew the secret of economy when he wrote, "That writer does the most who gives his reader the *most* knowledge, and takes from him the *least* time."

As you see in Figure 9-1, we're now at nine on the clock face, halfway through the revising stage of the writing process. Again, remember

Figure 9-1   Pay by the word.

Pay by the
Word

that revision tools are not rules, that you already have most of the revision tools you need, and most important, that revision tools are not drafting tools. To make your business writing more economical, do it as you revise, not as you draft. Don't interrupt the flow of that draft to worry about whether you've used too many words. Just put down the words as they come, even if you're going to cut some out later. American writer Truman Capote once said, "I believe more in the scissors than I do in the pencil."

OBJECTIVITY AND COMMON SENSE

Revising for economy is largely a matter of using two tools you already have: objectivity and common sense. After you've taken a break and returned to your draft as if you were reading it for the first time, you'll probably find ways to cut words. Just read each sentence and ask yourself, "Do I need to say this? If so, do I need to use this many words?" Sometimes, like Rex's owner in Figure 9-2, you'll realize that what you first wrote isn't really true.

Look at this sentence:

The part is blue in color.

Figure 9-2   Rex the dog.

Any writer could have drafted this sentence. But at the revising stage you realize that everyone knows that blue is a color. So revise the sentence to:

The part is blue.

The last two words of the original sentence added no meaning. They were already implied. Taking them off saves 33 percent—a savings any manager should be proud of.

Here's a similar sentence I've come across:

His mistakes were three (3) in number.

When I see this sentence, I'm tempted to say, "Not only does the writer not trust me to know that three is a number; he wants to make sure that I know which number it is." Double numbering has its place, on checks and other documents that need to be error proof and tamperproof, but there's absolutely no need for it in most business writing.

In his book *Claw Your Way to the Top*, humorist Dave Barry provided a helpful question and answer: "Q. What do they mean on the TV weather forecast when they say we are going to have 'thundershower activity'? A. They mean we are not going to have an actual thunderstorm, per se, but we are going to have thundershower activity, which looks very similar to the untrained eye."

As you revise, be sure to let your common sense work both ways—not only for deciding to cut unnecessary words but also for deciding to keep necessary ones.

TWO TOOLS

Besides objectivity and common sense, two easy grammatical tools can help you to manage your sentence economy. The first is what William Strunk Jr. and E. B. White, in their book *Elements of Style*, called "which-hunting." To go on a "which-hunt," look for each use of the words *which*, *that*, and *who* (or a form of *who*) in your draft. (If you know school grammar, what you're looking for is relative clauses; if that term doesn't mean anything to you, just ignore this sentence.) Some uses of these words are necessary, but some can be eliminated by rearranging the sentence. For example, you can change the phrase "a commission that consists of 10 members" into "a 10-member commission." In doing so, you've gotten rid of three words. But more important, you've eliminated a whole clause your reader won't need to process. The reader will subconsciously thank you.

Similarly, you can revise this sentence:

The state has vast deposits of coal that have not yet been developed.

into this one:

The state has vast undeveloped coal deposits.

The other grammatical tool involves looking for *prepositions*: the little words such as *of*, *in*, *on*, *with*, and *for* that indicate the relationship between the noun that follows and something else in the sentence. In business writing, the most common preposition is probably *of.*

Like *which*es, prepositions are often necessary, but they sometimes make a sentence uneconomical. For example, you can change:

> The fertilizer tablets are planted near the roots of the trees.

into:

> The fertilizer tablets are planted near the tree roots.

And sometimes you'll hit a jackpot, as in this sentence:

> The number of applications to schools of business is on the increase.

All four prepositions can be cut, leaving:

> Business school applications are increasing.

BECKWITH ON ECONOMY

Recently, one of the strongest champions of economical writing has been bestselling marketing guru Harry Beckwith. In his book *Selling the Invisible*, he wrote that vague, empty pieces of writing "tell your prospects one thing: They say you are willing to waste that person's time. No message can hurt you more." He continued, "Every prospect hopes you will heed the old New England proverb: 'Don't talk unless you can improve the silence.'"

And in his sequel, *The Invisible Touch*, Beckwith advised, "Skip the balderdash, the puffing, the filler: *Tell me.* Tell me the same way novelist Elmore Leonard (*Get Shorty*) writes books. Asked to explain why his books were so popular and so easy to read, Leonard answered: 'Simple. I just leave out the parts that readers skip.'"

Exercises

Exercise A

The following questions will test your understanding of this chapter. The final examination for this course will include similar questions.

1. Which of the following sentences is most economical without eliminating words that may carry important information?
    a. Textbook selection is accomplished through the use of a selection commission that consists of 10 members.
    b. Textbook selection is accomplished through the use of a 10-member selection commission.
    c. Textbooks are selected by a selection commission.
    d. Textbooks are selected by a 10-member commission.

2. Which of the following sentences is most economical without eliminating words that may carry important information?
    a. All unopened packages should be returned to the dock on 41st Street.
    b. All unopened packages should be returned to the 41st Street dock.
    c. All packages that are not opened should be returned to the dock on 41st Street.
    d. All packages that are not opened should be returned to the dock that is on 41st Street.

3. Which of the following sentences is most economical without eliminating words that may carry important information?
    a. Other factors that did not relate to an increased risk of cancer included . . .
    b. Other factors unrelated to an increased risk of cancer included . . .
    c. Other factors unrelated to an increased risk included . . .
    d. Other factors unrelated to an increased cancer risk included . . .

4. Which of the following sentences is most economical without eliminating words that may carry important information?
    a. The labels that are needed are rectangular in shape.
    b. The labels that are needed are rectangular.
    c. The needed labels are rectangular.
    d. The labels are rectangular.

5. Which of the following sentences is most economical without eliminating words that may carry important information?
   a. There are several projects that are successful which use volunteers.
   b. There are several successful projects that use volunteers.
   c. Several successful projects use volunteers.
   d. Several projects that are successful use volunteers.

6. Which of the following sentences is most economical without eliminating words that may carry important information?
   a. Please submit a report each week that lists all customer complaints.
   b. Please submit a report listing all customer complaints.
   c. Please submit a weekly report listing all customer complaints.
   d. Please submit a report each week listing all customer complaints.

7. Which of the following sentences is most economical without eliminating words that may carry important information?
   a. The agency will prepare a catalogue of the skills that each staff member possesses.
   b. The agency will catalogue each staff member's skills.
   c. The agency will prepare a catalogue of the skills of each staff member.
   d. The agency will prepare a catalogue of skills.

8. Which of the following sentences is most economical without eliminating words that may carry important information?
   a. The chairman will make a speech on the problems in marketing that the company has encountered.
   b. The chairman will speak on the problems in marketing that the company has encountered.
   c. The chairman will make a speech on the problems in marketing encountered by the company.
   d. The chairman will speak on the company's marketing problems.

9. Which of the following sentences is most economical without eliminating words that may carry important information?
   a. The costs of implementation will be offset by savings in time.
   b. The implementation costs will be offset by time savings.
   c. The costs of implementation will be offset by time savings.
   d. The implementation costs will be offset by savings in time.

10. Which of the following sentences is most economical without eliminating words that may carry important information?
    a. The process of writing has five (5) stages.
    b. The writing process has five (5) stages.
    c. The writing process has five stages.
    d. The process of writing has five stages.

Exercise B

Revise the following memo to make it more economical.

I am writing to inform all of you of all the details of our new vacation policy, which will replace the old vacation policy.

- Effective immediately, April 1, the anniversary of the birth of our founder, will be declared a company holiday. We are of the hope that the ultimate outcome of this extra day of released time will be an increase in the morale of the entire workforce.
- We have arranged with a travel agency for them to provide vacation opportunities at reduced prices for company employees. They have a brochure that is available in the Personnel Office which gives a complete listing of all the tours that are to be offered.
- It is required that all managers submit reports of employee vacation preferences once each quarter.

Thank you. If you have any questions on this new policy, please feel free to call on me personally at your convenience at any time.

MANAGE YOUR WRITING *TODAY*

On the very next writing job you have to do, begin with some writing management: Remind yourself that you're a writer, that writing can be managed, and that it's largely a matter of managing time. Set up blocks of time for planning, drafting, and revising—with more time allocated for planning and revising than for drafting.

- Then call in your Internal Editor to make the best possible "assignment" for this writing task. Begin by spending five minutes "finding the 'we.'" Take another five minutes to ask yourself, "What is the smallest community to which my audience and I both belong?" and "How are my audience and I alike and different in the four PACK dimensions: personality, attitude, circumstances, and knowledge?" Spend another five minutes to "make holes, not drills" by defining the purpose of the piece of writing. Take another five minutes or so to "get your stuff together," to gather information for the piece of writing. Then end the planning stage with five minutes of "getting your ducks in a row," organizing your information to best achieve your purpose for your reader(s).
- Next "do it wrong the first time." Bring in your Internal Writer to draft your document with as little interference as possible from your Internal Editor.
- Then take a break—for as long as you can, but for at least five minutes. Use this time to gain some objectivity about your draft and to "change hats" from your Internal Writer's rumpled fedora to your Internal Editor's eyeshade. When you return from the break, try to trick yourself into thinking that someone else wrote the draft, and look at it as if you're seeing it for the first time.
- Then revise your document using all the tools you already have in your toolbox, as well as the tools you've learned so far in this course. Pay special attention to "paying by the word," making your sentences as economical as possible.

When you've finished, take a few minutes to evaluate how the process worked for you. Evaluate especially whether paying by the word resulted in a more effective piece of writing at the end.

Remember, you really are paying by the word. Make sure that each word is worth what it costs you.

10

TRANSLATE INTO ENGLISH

Manage Your Word Choices

A s you see in Figure 10-1, we're coming up toward 10 on our watch, so we're just past halfway through the revising stage of the writing process. In Chapter 7 we learned a tool for revising paragraphs, and in Chapters 8 and 9 we learned two sets of tools for revising sentences. In this chapter we'll learn a powerful tool for revising individual words—a tool to use in this five-minute segment of the writing process.

Remember that our job as business writers is not to use words that mean the right thing to *us*. Our job is to find the best words to convey our meaning to our reader(s). That's why the revising stage is so important. It frees us from having to settle on the first word that came to our mind at the drafting stage. It gives us a chance to choose, from a number of possible words, the one word that best gets the job done. As Mark Twain said, "The difference between the right word and the almost right word is the difference between lightning and the lightning-bug." To choose the right word, we need the right tools.

An especially powerful tool is one I call "Translate into English." Naturally, this doesn't mean we need to translate from a foreign language. I mean that we need to translate from the kind of pseudo-English,

Figure 10-1   Translate into English.

Translate into
English

"official" English, that all of us sometimes write. David Weinberger, in *The Cluetrain Manifesto* (perhaps the most important book on business communication in the last couple of decades), called such pseudo-English "The Standard Style." Weinberger wrote, "Our business voice—in a managed environment—is virtually the same as everyone else's. . . . We learn to write memos in The Standard Style."

Take this letter, for example. It's one my dad received from a state women's basketball governing body. He had asked them about running an ad in their state tournament program.

Dear Mr. Davis:

Pursuant to your recent inquiry, please allow this communication to serve as reply thereto.

The Girls' State Basketball Tournament wherein the souvenir program is distributed commands an annual attendance of approximately 95,000 people. Additionally, we have a significant mailing to people in the middle west who purchase the program in advance for use while either hearing the games via radio or . . . .

And so it goes, for another page and a half.

Admittedly that's an extreme example of the kind of pseudo-English I'm talking about. But it's not *that* extreme. I'm sure it reminds you of many letters, memos, e-mail messages, and reports that you've received—or maybe even written.

That's an amazing fact about modern business. Some of the same people who like to think of themselves as on the cutting edge of technology, management theory, or marketing research still write the way people talked 200 years ago. They choose words that people haven't said to each other since they stopped wearing powdered wigs. When was the last time you heard a coworker say, "Pursuant to your recent inquiry"? Weinberger, again, wrote, "We have been trained throughout our business careers to suppress our individual voice and to sound like a 'professional,' that is, to sound like everyone else. This professional voice is distinctive. And weird. Taken out of context, it is as mannered as the ritualistic dialogue of the seventeenth-century French court."

Yet language almost that old-fashioned appears every day in business writing. The late Malcolm Forbes called it as he saw it: "Business jargon too often is cold, stiff, unnatural. Suppose I came up to you and said, 'I acknowledge receipt of your letter, and I beg to thank you.' You'd think, 'Huh?'"

Don't get me wrong. In the right place and time, there's nothing wrong with elegance in language. But if our purpose is to get something done, to make something happen, then we need to make sure—at the revising stage of our writing—that we use the most effective words possible. As Joseph Pulitzer advised, "Put it before them briefly so they will read it, clearly so they will appreciate it, picturesquely so they will remember it and, above all, accurately so they will be guided by its light."

LEARNING FROM THE IRS

Here are two examples of writing from the U.S. Internal Revenue Service (IRS). The first is from the instruction book for the 1040 Income Tax Form for 1976. (After you've read it, I'll tell you why I went back that far for an example.)

1976

The Privacy Act of 1974 provides that each Federal Agency inform individuals, whom it asks to supply information, of the authority for the solicitation of the information and whether disclosure of such information is mandatory or voluntary; the principal purpose or purposes for which the information is to be used; the routine uses which may be made of the information; and the effects on the individual of not providing the requested information. This notification applies to the U.S. Individual Income Tax Returns, to declarations of estimated tax, to U.S. Gift Tax returns, and to any other tax return required to be filed by an individual and to schedules, statements, or other documents related to the returns, and any subsequent inquiries necessary to complete, correct, and process the returns of taxpayers, to determine the correct tax liability and to collect any unpaid tax, interest, or penalty. . . .

The completion of all appropriate items requested by the return forms and related data is mandatory except for the Presidential Election Campaign Fund designation of the U.S. Individual Income Tax Returns, which is voluntary. . . .

Please retain this notification with your tax records and refer to it any time you are requested to furnish additional information.

In January 1977, just after the 1976 tax instructions were published, Jimmy Carter was sworn in as U.S. president. One of his first efforts from the White House was to make the language of government documents more effective. So in some areas of the government, really quick revisions were cranked out that first year. By January 1978, when the 1977 tax instructions were published, they had been greatly revised. Here's the same passage one year later:

1977

The Privacy Act of 1974 says that each Federal agency that asks for information must tell you the following:

1. Its legal right to ask for the information and whether the law says you must give it.
2. What purpose the agency has in asking for it, and the use to which it will be put.
3. What could happen if you do not give it.

For the Internal Revenue Service the law covers the following:

1. Tax returns and any papers you file with them.
2. Any questions we need to ask you so we can
    (a) complete, correct, or process your returns,
    (b) figure your tax, and
    (c) collect tax, interest or penalties. . . .

You must fill in all parts of the tax form that apply to you. But you do not have to check the boxes for the Presidential Election Campaign Fund. You can skip it if you wish. . . .

Please keep this notice with your records. It may help you if we ask you for other information.

These two samples say exactly the same thing. By law, they have to. We can be sure that before the 1977 revision was published, a whole troop of IRS lawyers signed off on it. But even though these versions say the same thing, the 1977 version is much, much easier to read and understand.

What kinds of improvements did the IRS make? Perhaps the most obvious is turning long sentences into outlines and lists. That's almost always a good idea. In the memos, letters, and reports we write, we should always look for ways to use numbered or bulleted lists instead of long sentences or paragraphs.

A second improvement is the use of "turn signals," the tool we learned in Chapter 7. Both the colon in the first sentence and the *but* near the end make the document easier to follow.

Another improvement is in the choice of subjects and verbs, the topic of Chapter 8. In one sentence, the subject and verb combination "completion is . . . mandatory" was changed to "you must fill in." And still another improvement is economy, as discussed in Chapter 9. The 1977 version is about 13 percent shorter.

However, the most important improvement may be less obvious. It occurs in individual words. More than a dozen words were replaced by simpler synonyms:

1976	1977
provides	says
inform	tell
individuals	you
authority	right
solicit	ask
provide	give
effects	what could happen
inquire	ask
complete	fill in
voluntary	you can skip
retain	keep
request	ask
additional	other

WORD HISTORIES

To understand the difference between the 1976 and 1977 lists, it may help to go back in history. (If you're not a history buff, feel free to skim this section.) The English language really began in the fifth century A.D. when tribes from what is now Denmark and northern Germany invaded Britain, pushing the native Celts back into Scotland, Ireland, and Wales. One of these tribes, the Angles, gave their name to the new country—Angle-land, or England—and to its language, which we now call Old English. When we look at something written in Old English (the great epic poem *Beowulf*, for example), it looks more like German than like modern English. And Germany, of course, is where it came from.

This Germanic language soon became widely used for government and business, as well as for everyday life. It lasted as the principal language of England until 1066, when a French duke, William of Normandy, crossed the English Channel with a French army and defeated the English army near a town called Hastings. William's victorious army marched into London, and on Christmas Day 1066, Duke William was crowned

King William, William I of England. He became known as William the Conqueror.

William and his conquering forces spoke a Latin-based language, an early form of French. So as he set up a new government over the conquered English, he imposed a new language on the country, as Figure 10-2 illustrates. For the next couple of centuries, both languages existed in England: French as the official language of government and business and English as the everyday language of most common people.

Gradually, the languages merged into what we now call Middle English, the language of Chaucer's *Canterbury Tales*. This language kept the structure and basic vocabulary of Old English but included a great number of French-origin words. Then, just as this merger was becoming complete, a new invasion came—not military this time but cultural. The Renaissance was spreading northward and westward from the Mediterranean. With its rebirth of learning and culture, it brought thousands of new French and Italian words. As a result of these two invasions—the military invasion of William the Conqueror and the cultural invasion of the Renaissance—English ended up with more words than any other language in the world.

Figure 10-2   The Norman Conquest.

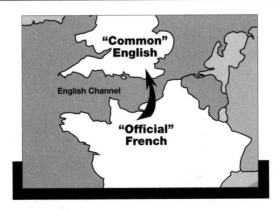

In activities such as farming that were untouched by either invasion, today's English words are largely Old English in origin. We often can recognize them as shorter and simpler. However, in certain activities, such as the performing arts, which had their rebirth in the Latin countries, our words are largely French or Italian in origin. They are often longer words. John Brunner, in his science fiction novel *The Shockwave Rider*, demonstrated this difference:

This is a basic place, a farm. Listen to it.

Land. House. Barn. Sun. Rain. Snow. Field. Fence. Pond. Corn. Wheat. Hay. Plow. Sow. Reap. Horse. Pig. Cow.

This is an abstract place, a concert hall. Listen to it.

Conductor. Orchestra. Audience. Overture. Concerto. Symphony. Podium. Harmony. Instrument. Oratorio. Variations. Arrangement. Violin. Clarinet. Piccolo. Tympani. Pianoforte. Auditorium.

As Brunner pointed out, you can "listen" to the difference between the two sets of words. The words in the "farm" list sound plainer; the words in the "concert hall" list sound fancier. Those in the first list are of Germanic origin. Forms of these words were used by English farmers before and after the Norman Conquest. Those in the second list are from French and Latin, brought in, as needed, to a society that had no native words for the stuff of concert halls.

A related pair of lists compares the words we use for kinds of meat and the animals they come from:

beef	cow
pork	pig, swine
mutton	sheep
venison	deer

In the years after the Norman Conquest, the people down at the barn taking care of the animals spoke Old English—so we get our animal names from them. The people around the table at the castle eating the good cuts of meat spoke French—so we get our meat names from them.

Many concepts, of course, were part of the language of both Old English and Norman French speakers. These include many common nouns, adjectives, adverbs, and (especially) verbs. As a result, Modern English has a very large number of synonyms from French/Latin and English/German sources. Here are some examples:

French/Latin	English/German
converse	talk
frequently	often
proceed	go
require	need
initial	first
dispatch	send
depart	leave
discover	find

An amazing fact, when you think about it, is that now, more than 900 years after the Norman Conquest, these two lists of words still carry a class difference. The French/Latin words still seem to us fancier and more "educated," just as the French-speaking officials must have seemed in the eleventh and twelfth centuries. The English/German words still seem to us plainer and less "educated," just as the Old English–speaking peasants must have seemed then.

As a result, the French/Latin words tend to find their way into "official" writing—the writing done in business, government, and the professions. Perhaps a desire to sound "official" caused the writers of the 1976 tax instructions to use so many French/Latin words. In fact, the 1976 word list above is made up entirely of French/Latin words.

This wouldn't be a problem except for one important fact: writing made up heavily of Latin-based words is more difficult to read. The longer Latin-based words slow down reading and lead to less understanding, even for well-educated readers. Germanic-origin words, on the other hand, make writing more readable. Even educated readers find these shorter, plainer words generally more effective. The revised 1977 list is made up entirely of words of Germanic origin.

The reason for the difference in readability does not lie so much in the history of our language as in the personal history of each individual reader. The English/German words are, in most cases, the ones we all learn first as children. The words in the previous right-hand lists are probably among the first thousand words an English-speaking child learns. When the child grows to adulthood, he or she continues to use these words most. One authority claims that all of the 100 most commonly used words in our language are of English/German origin. Thus it's no wonder that a passage such as the 1977 tax instructions made up of these simpler words will be read more easily and will communicate its content more effectively.

At this point you may be thinking, "Sure, you have to use simpler words in tax instructions because they have to be read by people with all levels of education, including grade-school dropouts. But if you're writing to someone with a lot more education, you should use bigger words."

Wrong. Even people with graduate and professional degrees will find the 1977 tax instructions easier to read than the 1976 instructions. No matter how much schooling we eventually get, the Germanic words remain more familiar, more easily accessible to our reading minds. Sonia Randhawa, writing at KMtalk, a Malaysian knowledge management site, said, "Bear in mind that your reader has a short attention span—or you have to presume that they do. Make life easy for them. Compress your information into concise, easy-to-read sentences. This doesn't mean that you're assuming that they're stupid, just that they're busy."

I've saved that last sentence to quote to clients when they think I'm telling them to "dumb down" their writing. Dumb has nothing to do with it. Even the most intelligent readers need clear, easy-to-read messages.

So a powerful tool for revising the words in your business writing is this: Unless you have a good reason otherwise, substitute plainer (English/German) words for fancier (French/Latin) words. In other words, "Translate into English."

You'll make your readers very happy. As "Rosa's Buzz-off Theory" (quoted in Paul Dickson's *The Official Rules*) states, "After completing that memo or report, substitute each buzz word with an everyday word. All on distribution will feel self-congratulatory at having for once understood a piece of writing in total. You will make friends."

The result also can have a direct payoff for your business. In his now-classic book on service marketing, *Selling the Invisible*, marketing guru Harry Beckwith wrote, "The famous direct-mail writer John Caples once changed one word in an ad—substituting 'fix' for 'repair'—and increased the response to the ad 20 percent." By now you should be able to recognize that the exact tool that Caples used was "Translate into English."

To use this tool, you certainly don't need to know German and French. You don't even need to look up word origins in a dictionary— although it sometimes can be interesting and fun to do so. (The *American Heritage Dictionary* is especially good for word origins.) All you have to do is substitute words that a child can understand, and your writing will be more readable, and more effective, for adult readers as well. As Fergus O'Connell wrote in *The Competitive Advantage of Common Sense*, "The key to being good at marketing is to be able to explain—very simply— why someone should buy what you sell. If you can tell it to me like I'm a six-year-old, then you will be a great marketer."

GOOD REASONS OTHERWISE

You may have noticed that the tool carries the qualification "unless you have a good reason otherwise." Sometimes you *will* have a good reason not to use this tool.

One possible reason is *precision*. Many fancier Latin-based words are necessary for their precise meaning. As Albert Einstein once said,

"Things should be made as simple as possible—but no simpler." The "concert hall" list showed that there are plenty of meanings for which no simple Germanic words exist. The Latin-based word *manufacture*, for example, once meant the same thing as the Germanic word *make*, but over the years, *manufacture* has taken on connotations of large-scale, mechanized "making" that give it a place of its own in our language. I *make* cookies; Keebler *manufactures* them. I *make* hamburgers; McDonald's *manufactures* them.

Sometimes, too, you will want to choose a fancier word for *variety*. If you have used *get* several times in a passage, you may want to substitute *obtain*, *secure*, or *acquire* sometimes. (This is why you may once have been taught to use longer words. At lower grade levels, it's important to expand our vocabulary.)

Finally, you may want to choose a Latin-based word for reasons of *courtesy* (a Latinate word itself, derived from the word for the king's *court*). You may sometimes find it more polite, for example, to *inform* people than to *tell* them.

Naturally, you may be concerned that using simpler words will make you seem less educated or less intelligent. But the great speakers and writers always have known that they are communicating to express, not impress. Ultimately, you must impress your reader or listener with your ideas, not your vocabulary, and a simple, direct vocabulary will help you to get those ideas across more effectively. Malcolm Forbes said it well: "Pretense invariably impresses only the pretender."

One of the great leaders—and great communicators—of the past century was British Prime Minister Winston Churchill. His speeches and writing gave courage to his nation during its most perilous time. But as someone once observed, think how ineffective Churchill would have been during World War II if he had said, "I have nothing to offer except hemoglobin, physical exertion, lachrymal secretions, and perspiration." No, what he said in his first statement as prime minister, on May 13, 1940, was, "I have nothing to offer except blood, toil, tears, and sweat." Churchill shared his secret when he wrote, in a sentence made up entirely of one-syllable, English-origin words, "Short words are best and the old words when short are best of all."

Churchill's friend and ally Franklin D. Roosevelt also was a master of "translating into English." According to Edward T. Thompson, former editor-in-chief of *Reader's Digest*, "A speech writer for President Franklin D. Roosevelt wrote, 'We are endeavoring to construct a more inclusive society.' FDR changed it to, 'We're going to make a country in which no one is left out.'"

You also may have to overcome an organizational culture that favors difficult language. But make sure you know what the expectations are. My late friend Kitty O. Locker, in her book *Business and Administrative Communication*, wrote, "If you think your boss doesn't want you to write simply, ask him or her. A few bosses do prize flowery language. Most don't."

Admittedly, some prejudices have to be overcome. William K. Zinsser, in his wonderful book *On Writing Well*, says, "Executives at every level are prisoners of the notion that a simple style reflects a simple mind. Actually, a simple style is the result of hard work and hard thinking; a muddy style reflects a muddy thinker or a person too lazy to organize his thoughts." And Patricia T. O'Conner and Stewart Kellerman, in their book *You Send Me*, noted that "Some puffed-up writers use long words, techie talk, trendy terms, and convoluted sentences to cover up or deceive or sound important or go along with the crowd. Most people who inflate their writing, though, are simply insecure, often for no good reason. They don't feel their ideas are strong enough, and they prop them up with elaborate language."

They continued, "If your ideas are any good, they can stand on their own. So kick away those unnecessary props. All they do is turn a strong writer into a wuss."

Similarly, Lee Woods, on his blog Smart People Write, said, "Bad writing makes smart people look dumb." Absolutely.

One of former Chrysler Chairman Lee Iacocca's "Eight Commandments of Good Management" is "Say it in English and keep it short."

Figure 10-3   The buzzword, management-style.

Chapter 9 gave tools for honoring the second part of Iacocca's commandment. In this chapter you've learned a powerful tool for honoring the first part: "Say it in English."

So maximize (to use cartoonist Jerry Van Amerongen's buzzword in Figure 10-3) the power of your writing by taking out words like *maximize*.

READABILITY FORMULAS AND STYLE CHECKERS

A number of readability formulas, both manual and computer-based, have been developed to measure the difficulty of written work. Perhaps the most widely used is part of the "grammar checker" built into Microsoft Word. It and some others claim to report the number of years of schooling required to read a document.

However, in the words of the U.S. Securities and Exchange Commission (SEC),

> You should be aware of a major flaw in every readability formula. No formula takes into account the content of the document being evaluated. In other words, no

formula can tell you if you have conveyed the information clearly. For the most part, they count the numbers of syllables and words in a sentence and the number of sentences in the sample. Of course, if you applied a readability formula to a traditional disclosure document, it would fail miserably. But keep in mind that by some formulas' calculations, Einstein's theory of relativity reads at a 5th grade level.

Some computerized style checkers analyze your grammar and identify the passive voice. They may suggest ways to make your writing more "readable." Take their suggestions as just that—suggestions. The final test of whether any piece of writing meets its goal of communicating information comes when humans read it.

If you would like some "numbers" on the readability of a draft, here's a simple tool you can use—a tool that takes an actual reader into account. This tool is based on the fact that at the level of sentences and words, the most readable writing is also the most predictable. Readable writing generally (not always, of course) fulfills the reader's expectations. Therefore, you can test the readability of a draft by hiding selected words and having a reader guess what they are. To run such a test:

1. Count back 50, 100, or 200 words from the end of your draft. (The exact number doesn't matter.)
2. Go through this ending and replace every fifth or every tenth word with a blank. Make all blanks the same length, regardless of the length of the words they replace.
3. Save this changed draft under a different name (so that you can get back to your original).
4. Have someone else read this copy of your draft and guess the missing words.
5. Note the "hits" and "misses," and decide whether each "miss" could have been a "hit" if it or words before it were changed. (Not all "misses" are bad things. Any writing will, and should, have *some* surprises.)
6. If you discover areas where rewriting is needed, do similar rewriting throughout your draft.

DELIBERATE "OBFUSCATION"?

Because fancy words can keep communication from happening, they can be used when you really don't want your message to be read and understood. One example may be the following recall notice from a car company that will remain anonymous:

> A defect which involves the possible failure of a frame support plate may exist on your vehicle. This plate (front suspension pivot bar support plate) connects a portion of the front suspension to the vehicle frame, and its failure could affect vehicle directional control, particularly during heavy brake application. In addition, your vehicle may require adjustment to the hood secondary catch system. The secondary catch may be misaligned so that the hood may not be adequately restrained to prevent hood fly-up in the event the primary catch is inadvertently left unengaged. Sudden hood fly-up beyond the secondary catch while driving could impair driver visibility. In certain circumstances, occurrence of either of the above conditions could result in vehicle crash without prior warning.

A cynic might read this notice and observe that the manufacturer complied with the law by sending out this document but didn't really want many people to bring in their cars for repair.

Here's another real-life example that I suspect is deliberate—though not for an unethical purpose. Rather, I suspect that a bored low-level soldier or civilian at the U.S. Department of Defense decided to test how far he or she could push bureaucratic jargon:

> 2.1.1 Specifications and standards
> Unless otherwise specified, the following specifications and standards of the issue listed in that issue of the Department of Defense Index of Specifications and Standards (DoDISS) specified in the solicitation, form a part of this specification to the extent specified herein.

Humorists have had a field day with this kind of language. Robert Thornton suggested, in his book *Lexicon of Intentionally Ambiguous*

Recommendations (*LIAR*, for short), that when we write recommendation letters, we actually might *want* to use confusing language. Among his examples are the following:

> "You'll be lucky to get him to work for you."
> "He doesn't mind being disturbed."
> "He's a man of many convictions."
> "You simply won't believe this woman's credentials."
> "I most enthusiastically recommend this man with no qualifications whatsoever."

Dave Barry, in *Claw Your Way to the Top*, advised, "Use the word 'transpire' a lot. Wrong: The dog barked. Right: What transpired was, the dog barked. Even better: A barking of the dog transpired."

On the Web, Mike Shor developed a tool called "MBA-Writer" for automatically generating "sentences ready for inclusion into your business memos without all of the thinking." Here are the first three sentences it generated for me:

- Realigning core competencies, the asynchronous transitional capability internalizes an enterprise-wide value framework.
- Within an impactful environment, leveraging customer positions collaboratively and interdependently disseminates the shifting of age-old paradigms.
- In layman's terms, our contingency schematic requires further offline considerations of multiproduct decisioning.

And *Dilbert* creator Scott Adams wrote, "If you want to advance in management, you have to convince other people that you're smart. This is accomplished by substituting incomprehensible jargon for common words. For example, a manager would never say, 'I used my fork to eat a potato.' A manager would say, 'I utilized a multitined tool to process a starch resource.' The two sentences mean almost the same thing, but the second one is obviously from a smarter person."

Seriously, you have to make the ethical decision about which way to use this tool. You can use it to change plain words to fancy ones in order to hide their meaning. However, if you truly want to get your message across, "Translate into English."

THREE EXAMPLES

Before we get to the exercises for this chapter, I want to show you three examples of simple, powerful business writing, all taken from *The Forbes Book of Great Business Letters*. First is an 1848 letter (in its entirety) from business giant Cornelius Vanderbilt to his former agents:

> You have undertaken to cheat me. I won't sue you, for the law is too slow. I'll ruin you.

The second is from a memo from Roger Enrico, president and CEO of Pepsi-Cola USA, to all bottlers and employees. The year was 1985. The occasion was rival Coca-Cola's introduction of New Coke:

> There is no question the long-term market success of Pepsi has forced this move. Everyone knows when something is right it doesn't need changing. Maybe they finally realized what most of us have known for years . . . Pepsi tastes better than Coke.

The third is from a message from Tom Paquin, manager at Netscape, encouraging engineers to meet a release deadline:

> We do whatever it takes. And feel damn great about it when we pull it off.

As sports agent Mark H. McCormack wrote, "Short words, short sentences, short paragraphs work. Trust me."

Exercises

Exercise A

The following questions will test your understanding of this chapter. The final examination for this course will include similar questions.

1. Which of the following sentences uses words most effectively?
   a. The report is intended to provide information on a monthly basis to senior management and others as necessary.
   b. The report is meant to provide monthly information to senior management and others as necessary.
   c. The report is intended to provide information on a monthly basis to senior management and needed others.
   d. The report will get monthly information to senior managers and others.

2. Which of the following sentences uses words most effectively?
   a. As we examine our position in relation to supporting the fund drive, it seems that we will be unable to participate at the same level we did in 2004.
   b. We won't be able to give as much to the fund drive as we did in 2004.
   c. As we examine our position in relation to supporting the fund drive, it seems that we will be unable to contribute at the same level we did in 2004.
   d. As we review our position in relation to supporting the fund drive, it appears that we will be unable to participate at the same level we did in 2004.

3. Which of the following sentences uses words most effectively?
   a. The above information provides necessary information in evaluating the extent of opportunity available.
   b. The above information provides information necessary for the evaluation of the extent of opportunity available.
   c. This information tells us what we need to make a decision.
   d. This information is necessary for evaluating the extent of opportunity available.

4. **Which of the following sentences uses words most effectively?**
    a. After reviewing the data, we will talk with you about what happens next.
    b. After reviewing the data, we will be in contact with you to determine next steps as warranted.
    c. After reviewing the data, we will be in contact with you to determine next steps.
    d. After reviewing the data, we will contact you to determine next steps as warranted.

5. **Which of the following sentences uses words most effectively?**
    a. We did not attempt to estimate the potential negative effect on our business.
    b. We did not attempt to estimate the potential negative impact on our business.
    c. We did not attempt to calculate the potential negative effect on our business.
    d. We did not try to estimate the potential harm to our business.

6. **Which of the following sentences uses words most effectively?**
    a. If you agree, please contact the Foundation and advise them that you are our company's representative and that all future correspondence should be directed to you.
    b. If you agree, please tell the Foundation that you are our representative and ask them to send all mail to you.
    c. If you agree, please contact the Foundation and tell them that you are our company's representative and that all future correspondence should be sent to you.
    d. If you agree, please contact the Foundation and tell them that you are our company's representative and request that they direct all future correspondence to you.

7. **Which of the following sentences uses words most effectively?**
    a. I would like for you to investigate the feasibility of managing the timely clearance of priority items from your area.
    b. I would like for you to look into the feasibility of managing the timely clearance of priority items from your area.
    c. Please investigate the feasibility of managing the timely clearance of priority items from your area.
    d. Please look into how you can clear priority items on time.

8. Which of the following sentences uses words most effectively?
    a. The chairman will present a speech on the difficulties in marketing that the company has encountered.
    b. The chairman will speak on the difficulties in marketing that the company has encountered.
    c. The chairman will make a speech on the problems in marketing encountered by the company.
    d. The chairman will speak on the company's marketing problems.
9. Which of the following sentences uses words most effectively?
    a. The Girls' State Basketball Tournament wherein the souvenir program is distributed commands an annual attendance of approximately 95,000 people.
    b. The Girls' State Basketball Tournament, where the souvenir program is distributed, draws about 95,000 people each year.
    c. The Girls' State Basketball Tournament wherein the souvenir program is distributed draws an attendance of approximately 95,000 people annually.
    d. The Girls' State Basketball Tournament, where the souvenir program is distributed, commands an annual attendance of about 95,000 people.
10. Which of the following sentences uses words most effectively?
    a. The process of written composition possesses five successive stages.
    b. The process of written composition has five stages.
    c. The writing process has five stages.
    d. The process of written composition possesses five stages.

Exercise B

Revise the following memo to make its words simpler and more effective:

As I've conversed with many of you over the past several months, I've frequently heard you inquire, "Are we attempting to manufacture too many new products? Do we really require such an extensive line?"

My initial response is to emphasize the importance of altering our company's image. To obtain our share of the market, we must rectify the faults of the past. We must be perceived as a company willing to institute innovations and progress into new areas.

I'm confident that if you scrutinize the matter, you will discover that I am correct.

MANAGE YOUR WRITING *TODAY*

On the very next writing job you have to do, begin with some writing management: Remind yourself that you're a writer, that writing can be managed, and that it's largely a matter of managing time. Set up blocks of time for planning, drafting, and revising—with more time allocated for planning and revising than for drafting.

- Then call in your Internal Editor to make the best possible "assignment" for this writing task. Begin by spending five minutes "finding the 'we.'" Take another five minutes to ask yourself, "What is the smallest community to which my audience and I both belong?" and "How are my audience and I alike and different in the four PACK dimensions: personality, attitude, circumstances, and knowledge?" Spend another five minutes to "make holes, not drills" by defining the purpose of the piece of writing. Take another five minutes or so to "get your stuff together," to gather information for the piece of writing. Then end the planning stage with five minutes of "getting your ducks in a row," organizing your information to best achieve your purpose for your reader(s).
- Now "do it wrong the first time." Bring in your Internal Writer to draft your document with as little interference as possible from your Internal Editor.
- Then take a break—for as long as you can, but for at least five minutes. Use this time to gain some objectivity about your draft and to "change hats" from your Internal Writer's rumpled fedora to your Internal Editor's eyeshade.
- When you return from the break, try to trick yourself into thinking that someone else wrote the draft, and look at it as if you're seeing it for the first time. Then revise your document using all the tools you already have in your toolbox, as well as the tools you've learned so

far in this book. Pay special attention to "translating into English," making your words as simple as possible—but, as Einstein said—not more so.

When you've finished, take a few minutes to evaluate how the process worked for you. Evaluate especially whether translating into English resulted in a more effective piece of writing at the end.

11

FINISH THE JOB
Manage Your Spelling, Punctuation, and Mechanics

What are your biggest communication problems? When I asked this question of several hundred businesspeople, their number one answer was "speaking to a group," followed by "being persuasive in my speaking and writing." But high on the list—in fact, the highest problem on the list specific to writing—was "using correct spelling and punctuation."

I call this "finishing the job." I've chosen the phrase carefully to take advantage of the two ways we use the verb *finish*: to mean "end" (as in "I've finished the work") and to mean "put a surface on" (as in "I've finished this table with varnish").

The first meaning of *finish* is important for our purpose because, as shown in Figure 11-1, spelling and punctuation should be the *end* of our writing process, the last thing we think about before sending the letter, memo, or report to our reader(s). Most of us worry about spelling and punctuation much too early in the writing process. As a result, several bad things happen:

- We interrupt the flow of our drafting.
- We waste time correcting words and sentences we might later decide not to use at all.
- We commit ourselves to the concept of perfection too early, thus blinding ourselves to changes that really might need to be made.

So we need to remind ourselves that spelling and punctuation are the way we *finish* the process.

The second meaning of *finish* is also important for our purpose, because spelling and punctuation are nothing more or less than the *finish*, or surface, on a piece of writing. On one hand, this makes them very important: they're the first thing our reader sees and judges us on. As Mark H. McCormack wrote in *What They* Still *Don't Teach You at Harvard Business School*, "Only sloppy executives send out sloppy memos. Perfect grammar and perfect proofreading display professionalism and courtesy to the reader. Even if your suggestions are shot down, you will earn credibility." The late Malcolm Forbes said it too: "Make it perfect. No typos, no misspellings, no factual errors. If you're sloppy and let mistakes slip by, the person reading your letter will think you don't know better or don't care. Do you?"

Figure 11-1   Finish the job.

On the other hand, the fact that spelling and punctuation are just *finish* keeps their importance in perspective. Just as a shiny coat of paint can't make up for a badly engineered or badly built car underneath, so a perfect spelling and punctuation job can't make up for a badly conceived or written letter.

One reason most English speakers (including me) think of ourselves as poor spellers may be a frustration at those endless spelling tests we all took in school. But there's a more important reason for our insecurity—and it's not our fault. We English speakers have inherited what is almost surely the world's most difficult language to spell.

Speakers of Spanish, Russian, or Japanese have much less trouble with spelling. Their languages have developed more straightforwardly, with a neater fit between spelling and pronunciation. English, however, doesn't have such a neat fit, and so it *causes* fits. English developed in twists and turns, absorbing elements from various other languages at various times. Moreover, it developed the idea of consistent spelling late. A seventeenth-century merchant might even have spelled his own name differently from one day to the next. Even Shakespeare seems to have done so.

Thus English has become a nightmare of spelling quirks. Imagine someone trying to learn our language. She is told that the word *cough* is pronounced "coff"; *tough*, however, is not "toff," but "tuff." Add an *h* to make it *though*, and you get "thoff"? No. "thuff"? No. "thoe"! And inserting an *r* to make it *through* gives you a fourth sound, "threw."

We native speakers usually don't have trouble with these words. Our problem is not with spellings that produce multiple sounds but with sounds that have multiple or unusual spellings. Our problems are with *ie* and *ei*, with *ance* and *ence*, and with single and double consonants. No wonder we are bad spellers.

Yet, for a people who *are* bad spellers, we Americans are not especially forgiving of bad spelling by each other. We businesspeople, in particular, single out spelling more than anything else when getting a first impression of a piece of writing. Two or three misspelled words in an otherwise brilliant job application letter can doom that letter to the waste-basket faster than anything else. Reporter Bob Considine framed what he calls "Considine's Law": "Whenever one word or letter can change the entire meaning of a sentence, the probability of an error being made will be in direct proportion to the embarrassment it will cause."

So what's the answer? Here are several:

- **When you write with a computer, use a spelling checker.** Most word processing programs and even some typewriters now come with built-in dictionaries, and they can save you a lot of time and embarrassment. Remember, though, to spell-check only *after* you have written a draft, not *while* you are drafting. Interrupting a draft to worry about spelling can take your attention away from more important concerns (so turn off that on-the-fly spell-checker in Microsoft Word). Remember, too, that spelling checkers don't relieve you of the responsibility of improving your spelling skills. For one thing, they can't catch all errors, especially errors that result in real words with different meanings, such as *there* and *three*. For another, most of us still do lots of writing without a computer: forms and handwritten messages, for example.

- **Proofread carefully.** Use the professional proofreader's trick of reading your writing backward, a word at a time. Starting from the end and reading to the beginning forces you to see each word *as a word*, not as part of a larger meaning. And of course, whenever possible, ask someone else to proofread for you. You can return the favor.

- **When in doubt, look it up.** Keep a good dictionary on your desk, and use it often. (Be sure to get a reputable, up-to-date dictionary. See Appendix D for recommendations.)

- **Track your spelling problems.** When you look up a word, put a tick mark beside it in your dictionary. Do the same when your spelling checker finds a mistake. You'll build your own inventory of words you need to learn.

- **Consider learning three or four spelling rules.** If your problems are with *ie* and *ei* or with what to do with *y*, silent *e*, or single consonants when adding suffixes, there are rules that can help. You can get them from many handbooks.
- **Make up your own tricks.** When a word repeatedly gives you trouble, make up the silliest, most juvenile trick you can for it. As a teacher and trainer, I often have to write the word *attendance*, but I could never remember whether it ended with *ance* or *ence* until someone told me to remember "Attendance at a dance." So now that's what goes through my mind every time I write the word. Laugh if you want, but the trick saves me from looking it up.

These tips won't make you a perfect speller. Given the nature of our language, few people ever spell perfectly. With a little effort, though, you can reduce your errors considerably.

The bad news about *punctuation* is that it is even less standardized than spelling. Each English-speaking country, each profession, each publication, and even each company seems to have its own official or unofficial rules about what and how to punctuate when. The best advice about this diversity of rules, therefore, is to find out if the company or publication you're writing for has an official style sheet, and stick to it.

The *good* news about punctuation is that there is much less to learn about it than about spelling. English has hundreds of thousands of words but fewer than a dozen commonly used punctuation marks. So begin paying attention to them and turning to a handbook when you need help. Soon you'll be competing confidently with Graham in the Emphatic Punctuation Contest (Figure 11-2).

Together, a few punctuation rules and the spelling tips listed earlier may give you more skill and confidence as a writer. They can't turn bad writing into good, but they may help you put those important finishing touches on an already good document.

Figure 11-2   Graham is an easy winner in the "period" category.

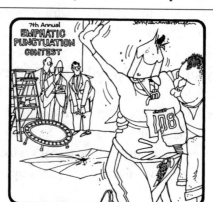

Exercise

The final examination for this course will include questions similar to the following. As you answer these questions, remember that they're diagnostic, designed to include some of the most common spelling and punctuation problems. Pay attention to the correct answers to the questions you miss. They will tell you what you especially need to work on.

1. Which of the following sentences is most conventional in spelling, punctuation, and mechanics?
   a.   Please return the voltmeter to its case.
   b.   Please return the voltmeter to it's case.
   c.   Please return the voltmeter to its' case.
   d.   None of these answers uses conventional spelling.

2. Which of the following sentences is most conventional in spelling, punctuation, and mechanics?
   a.   In his letter to us, he said that our proposal was alot of "hot air".
   b.   In his letter to us, he said that our proposal was a lot of "hot air".
   c.   In his letter to us, he said that our proposal was alot of "hot air."
   d.   In his letter to us, he said that our proposal was a lot of "hot air."

3. **Which of the following sentences is most conventional in spelling, punctuation, and mechanics?**
   a. When will the new stationary be printed?
   b. When will the new stationery be printed?
   c. When will the new stationary be printted?
   d. When will the new stationery be printted?

4. **Which of the following sentences is most conventional in spelling, punctuation, and mechanics?**
   a. The new tax law will effect our accounting system; it also will have a major affect on our tax flow.
   b. The new tax law will effect our accounting system; it also will have a major effect on our tax flow.
   c. The new tax law will affect our accounting system; it also will have a major affect on our tax flow.
   d. The new tax law will affect our accounting system; it also will have a major effect on our tax flow.

5. **Which of the following sentences is most conventional in spelling, punctuation, and mechanics?**
   a. Abu Dhabi is the capitol and principle city of the United Arab Emirates.
   b. Abu Dhabi is the capitol and principal city of the United Arab Emirates.
   c. Abu Dhabi is the capital and principle city of the United Arab Emirates.
   d. Abu Dhabi is the capital and principal city of the United Arab Emirates.

6. **Which of the following sentences is most conventional in spelling, punctuation, and mechanics?**
   a. She has already read your letter and says your suggestion is alright with her.
   b. She has already read your letter and says your suggestion is all right with her.
   c. She has all ready read your letter and says your suggestion is alright with her.
   d. She has all ready read your letter and says your suggestion is all right with her.

7. **Which of the following sentences is most conventional in spelling, punctuation, and mechanics?**
   a. I'm sure you've perceived the new title occuring after my name.
   b. I'm sure you've perceived the new title occurring after my name.
   c. I'm sure you've percieved the new title occuring after my name.
   d. I'm sure you've percieved the new title occurring after my name.

8. Which of the following sentences is most conventional in spelling, punctuation, and mechanics?

    a. In retracing his path, the courier was worryed that he might have omitted something.

    b. In retracing his path, the courier was worried that he might have omitted something.

    c. In retraceing his path, the courier was worryed that he might have omited something.

    d. In retraceing his path, the courier was worried that he might have omited something.

9. Which of the following sentences is most conventional in spelling, punctuation, and mechanics?

    a. The flag is red, green, white, and black.

    b. The flag is red, green, white and black.

    c. Both *a* and *b* are conventional.

    d. Neither *a* nor *b* is conventional.

10. Which of the following sentences is most conventional in spelling, punctuation, and mechanics?

    a. Did she complete the form marked "Secret"?

    b. Did she complete the form marked "Secret?"

    c. "Where do we go from here?" he asked.

    d. Both *a* and *c* are correct.

MANAGE YOUR WRITING *TODAY*

On the very next writing job you have to do, begin with some writing management: Remind yourself that you're a writer, that writing can be managed, and that it's largely a matter of managing time. Set up blocks of time for planning, drafting, and revising—with more time allocated for planning and revising than for drafting.

- Then call in your Internal Editor to make the best possible "assignment" for this writing task. Begin by spending five minutes "finding the 'we.'" Take another five minutes to ask yourself, "What is the smallest community to which my audience and I both belong?" and "How are my audience and I alike and different in the four PACK dimensions: personality, attitude, circumstances, and knowledge?" Spend another five minutes to "make holes, not drills" by defining the purpose of the piece of writing. Take another five minutes or so to "get your stuff together," to gather information for the piece of writing. Then end the planning stage with five minutes of "getting your ducks in a row," organizing your information to best achieve your purpose for your reader(s).

- Now "do it wrong the first time." Bring in your Internal Writer to draft your document with as little interference as possible from your Internal Editor.

- Then take a break—for as long as you can, but for at least five minutes. Use this time to gain some objectivity about your draft and to "change hats" from your Internal Writer's rumpled fedora to your Internal Editor's eyeshade.

- When you return from the break, try to trick yourself into thinking that someone else wrote the draft, and look at it as if you're seeing it for the first time. Then revise your document using all the tools you already have in your toolbox, as well as the tools you've learned so far in this course. Finish the revising stage by "finishing" the document, putting a professional surface on it with correct spelling, punctuation, and other mechanics.

When you've done that, take a few minutes to evaluate how the process worked for you. Evaluate especially whether "finishing the job" resulted in a more effective piece of writing at the end.

12

MANAGE YOUR WRITING

Evaluate Your Writing Process

Good managers know the importance of evaluating their work. As a manager of your own writing, you need to end each writing "hour" (as shown in Figure 12-1) with two or three minutes of evaluation—not of the written *product* (your Internal Editor has been doing that throughout the revising stage), but of your writing *process*. Which stages of the process needed more time than you gave them? Which stages needed less?

Like the hands on a clock, the writing process doesn't stop with each cycle. It's a continuous process. The evaluation you do at the end of one writing job can help you be a better manager at the beginning of the next.

I'm certainly not saying that your writing can become as mechanized as the writing of the executive at Ace Conveyor Company in Figure 12-2. But I am saying that in the past 36 hours you have learned a process that can help you manage and streamline your writing process in the same way that engineers learn to streamline any other production process.

Figure 12-1   Manage your writing.

And through this recurring process, evaluated at the end of each cycle, you'll continue to grow as a writer for the rest of your life. You'll have learned to *manage your writing.*

MANAGE YOUR WRITING *TODAY*

On the very next writing job you have to do, begin with some writing management: Remind yourself that you're a writer, that writing can be managed, and that it's largely a matter of managing time. Set up blocks

Figure 12-2   Ace Conveyor Co.

of time for planning, drafting, and revising—with more time allocated for planning and revising than for drafting.

- Then call in your Internal Editor to make the best possible "assignment" for this writing task. Begin by spending five minutes "finding the 'we.'" Take another five minutes to ask yourself, "What is the smallest community to which my audience and I both belong?" and "How are my audience and I alike and different in the four PACK dimensions: personality, attitude, circumstances, and knowledge?" Spend another five minutes to "make holes, not drills" by defining the purpose of the piece of writing. Take another five minutes or so to "get your stuff together," to gather information for the piece of writing. Then end the planning stage with five minutes of "getting your ducks in a row," organizing your information to best achieve your purpose for your reader(s).
- Next "do it wrong the first time." Bring in your Internal Writer to draft your document with as little interference as possible from your Internal Editor.
- Then take a break—for as long as you can, but for at least five minutes. Use this time to gain some objectivity about your draft and to "change hats" from your Internal Writer's rumpled fedora to your Internal Editor's eyeshade.
- When you return from the break, try to trick yourself into thinking that someone else wrote the draft, and look at it as if you're seeing it for the first time. Then revise your document using all the tools you already have in your toolbox, as well as the tools you've learned so far in this book. Finish the revising stage by "finishing" the document, putting a professional surface on it with correct spelling, punctuation, and other mechanics.

When you've done that, take a few minutes to evaluate how the process worked for you. Did you take enough time at each stage? Too much time? Finally, evaluate whether managing your writing process resulted in a more effective piece of writing at the end.

APPENDIX X

MANAGE YOUR ONLINE WRITING

In the early 1980s, when word processing software began to appear, Stewart Brand, father of the *Whole Earth Catalog*, called word processing the "technology I've been waiting half a lifetime for." Well, one short wait for that writer was one long wait for humankind. In the past 25 years, we have begun to use the most important new writing tool since the stylus—in fact, the only significantly new writing technology in 8,000 years—the personal computer.

Computer—what an ugly and misleading word. Von Neumann, back in the 1940s, had a better idea: he called the thing an "all-purpose machine." And the French, as usual, have a good word for it: *ordinateur*—the machine that orders, that organizes, that arranges. But *computer?* The word reduces one of humanity's most far-reaching inventions to a merely mathematical device.

Now don't get me wrong. I'm appropriately grateful to the mathematicians, engineers, and computer scientists who have worked to give us this tool. But they have done more than many of them know. The lasting value of their creation may lie not in helping humanity to *compute* but in helping humanity to *write.*

THE WRITING MACHINE

Humanity has been writing, archeologists tell us, since about 6000 B.C. As I mentioned briefly in the Introduction, the first writers discovered that written language has several advantages over spoken language:

- It can be absorbed more quickly.
- It can be scanned with the eyes.
- It can be consulted later.
- It can be passed with confidence from messenger to messenger.

All these advantages are results of writing's relative *permanence*. But the very permanence that gives writing these advantages has traditionally made the process of creating it very difficult.

- First, the physical act of representing an idea by a permanent squiggle—on stone, papyrus, slate, or paper—is so hard that few of us get really good at it. (Thank goodness you're not trying to read this book in my handwriting.) As a textbook once proclaimed in its title, writing is an unnatural act.
- And second, once we've made such a permanent squiggle, we're reluctant to change it.

As a result, most of us have worked very hard to get all those squiggles right the first time so that we don't have to do them again. As Figure I-1 in the Introduction illustrates, we agonize our way down the page, carefully considering each squiggle before we write it—planning, drafting, and editing all at once. And when the draft is finished, *we're* finished: the permanence of the squiggles traditionally has made us reluctant to look at them again (the literal meaning of *revise*) with an eye toward improvement.

The computer changes all this. It still gives us a permanent written product—on paper or disk—with all the advantages that permanence has had for 8,000 years. But—and this is important—it allows us to postpone the permanence until we want it, at the very end of the writing process. Until then, we can write on the most impermanent of media: a video screen.

The implications of this fact are profound at each stage of the writing process. At what this book calls the planning stage, we can begin by jotting down fragmentary ideas, copying notes from other sources, and roughing out possible organizational patterns. But with the computer, we can manipulate these jottings much more freely, arranging and combining them in new ways. And even more wonderfully, once we key in a word or phrase, we need never do so again, unless we wish to. Our preliminary jottings can become an actual part of our final document, in a way they never could when we wrote on paper.

As we move into the drafting stage of the process, we can, if we wish, open our planning work in one on-screen window as we draft in another. When it's more efficient to move a phrase from one window to another than it is to rekey it, we can do that. And the anticipated ease of revision lets us draft much more freely and spontaneously than before, with much less constraint from what Chapter 6 calls our Internal Editor.

It's at the revising stage that the computer really proves its worth as a writing machine. It allows us to do all the kinds of revising we could do on paper—deleting, inserting, and changing—but after each of these operations, we immediately have a "clean" copy of the document, not the very "dirty," marked-up copy we used to have. We can see exactly what we've done, instead of having to imagine it, so we can make wiser editorial decisions.

The computer also permits other kinds of revision that simply weren't possible on paper. A single command takes us to any given word. Another swaps any word or phrase for any other, either at all places it occurs or at those we select. And so on. When we're finally satisfied—or out of time—we can run the spell-check. (And I beg you to turn off the feature in your word processor that checks spelling as you type. Save spell-schecking for step 11.)

For all these reasons, the writing machine (call it a computer if you insist) directly supports and encourages the five-stage writing process that will make us more effective and efficient writers. With it, we have no excuse to remain sentence-by-sentence, "one-stage" writers.

FOUR CHALLENGES

This book's introduction pointed out what you surely already knew: not only is most writing being done on computer, but more and more writing is also being *read* on computer screens—in the form of e-mail and Web pages. All the tools you've learned so far in this book certainly apply to online writing as much as they do to writing that's read on paper. But online writing brings its own special challenges. In this appendix we'll look at four of those challenges and the ways we writers must respond to them.

The four challenges of online writing are shown in the left column of Figure A-1. They remind us that online writing is—or should be—screen-based, interactive, global, and immediate. Each of these challenges has implications:

- Implications for the *"texture"* of writing (its words, sentences, and paragraphs—the things we've learned to pay special attention to throughout the revising stage)
- Implications for the *structure* of writing (its overall organization—which we learned to pay special attention to at the end of the planning stage)

The first challenge of online writing is that it appears on-screen. And according to Web usability expert Jakob Nielsen, screen-based reading (for now, at least) is 25 percent slower than paper-based reading. So as Figure A-1 points out, online writing should be especially concise. To use the language of Chapter 9, it should be especially *economical* because you're "paying" a lot for each word. Nielsen also has found that 79 percent of online readers scan rather than truly read. So online writing should be

Figure A-1   Manage your online writing.

Online writing should be ▼	In texture	In structure
Screen-based	• concise • highlighted	• visibly structured • "fronted"
Interactive	• informatively linked	• "chunked" (but not linearly)
Global	• multilingual, if possible • in "world English"	• multistructured, if possible (deductive and inductive)
Immediate	• personal • objective, not "rhetorical"	• conversational • narrative
Manage Your Online Writing		

highlighted—with key words, sentences, or ideas in italic or boldface, for example.

Just as the *texture* of online writing has to meet the challenge of screen-based reading, so does its *structure*. Because online readers tend to scan, a Web page or e-mail message should be visibly structured; it should have what Nielsen calls a "scannable layout." He found that frequent use of headings and bullets can increase readability by 47 percent. And since his study found that only about 10 percent of online readers scroll below the text initially visible on the screen, online writing should be "fronted," with the most important information placed at the beginning. Unless you have a good reason otherwise—as in a "bad news" message, for example—structure your Web pages and e-mail messages like newspaper articles, with the most important information in the headline (or subject line) and the first paragraph.

The second challenge of online writing is that it should be interactive. Words on paper can't appear or disappear immediately at the reader's command, but words on a computer screen can. So readers of online text increasingly expect it to be interactive. Therefore online writing should be informatively linked, giving its readers clear choices about where to go next. As Nielsen said, "The departure page must include sufficient information to enable users to decide what link to follow next." He adds that link titles should include "details about the kind of information to be found on the destination page, as well as how it relates to the anchor text and to the context of the current page."

Making online text interactive requires "chunking" it, that is, splitting it into shorter passages. These chunks, however, should not be merely linear, turning the computer into nothing more than an expensive page-turning machine. Readers expect that online writing, especially Web-based writing, will give them true choices that are networked rather than linear (compare Figures 4-1 and 4-2 in Chapter 4).

The third challenge of online writing is that it should be global. The universality of the Web means that readers can come from dozens or hundreds of cultures. And even an e-mail message to one person can easily be forward to many more around the world. So if you want or expect a global readership for your writing, especially on Web pages, consider making it multilingual. If you can't get it translated into multiple languages, at least translate it yourself into "world" English—English that relies on relatively simple words and sentences and that avoids analogies specific to one culture, such as the doughnuts and muffins of Chapter 1. Naturally, by translating your draft into "world" English, you'll almost always be making it more effective for native English speakers within your own culture as well.

Besides requiring simpler words and sentences, global readers also come to your writing with different structural preferences and expectations. Ronald Scollon and Suzanne Wong Scollon, in their book *Intercultural Communication*, reminded us that some readers prefer deductive organization, with the topic "introduced at the beginning so that it will be clear what the relevance of the supporting arguments is." Other readers prefer inductive organization, with the supporting arguments first, building up to a conclusion. Although both patterns are used in all societies, some societies may have a general preference for one or the other. The interactive nature of the Web gives us the opportunity to create multistructured text, with both deductive and inductive options for our readers.

The fourth challenge of online writing is that readers expect it to be immediate—without "mediation." As the writers of *The Cluetrain Manifesto* said, "The Internet became a place where people could talk to other people without constraint. Without filters or censorship or official sanction." So the texture of online writing should be personal, not bureaucratic. Nielsen's research found that on Web pages, "what's respected is the presence of a clear voice." *The Cluetrain Manifesto*, again, talks about *voices*, comparing the *business* voice, "virtually the same as everyone else's," with the *personal* voice, the "strongest, most direct expression of who we are."

Similarly, online writing generally should be objective, not hyped. As Nielsen said, "The Web is a rather 'cool' medium that encourages the use of facts with links to back-up datasheets and detailed numbers. You cannot get away with the superficial hyperbole that may work in television commercials or magazine advertising."

In its structure, online writing should meet the challenge of immediacy by being conversational, by respecting the reader's time by being relevant, by providing as much information as the reader needs but no more, and by telling the truth.

Online writing also should make extensive use of narratives—of stories. Stories have always been important in forming communities and organizations. As *The Cluetrain Manifesto* reminded us, "Stories play a large part in the success of organizations. With stories, we teach, pass along knowledge of our craft to colleagues, and create a sense of shared mission." Bran Ferren, an executive vice president of Walt Disney Imagineering, told a writer for *CIO Web Business Magazine*, "The Web is a storytelling medium. Most people function in a storytelling mode. It's the way we communicate ideas, richly." He continued, "The deeper memory of an organization has to do with the sense of community, colleagues functioning together, history, accomplishments and so forth. All of that ultimately makes up the culture of a corporation. Part of the issue is how to convey that to the outside world. Information technology is now being used to do that in the Web pages that many companies are now using, and they're doing it incredibly badly because they're not taking it seriously as a storytelling problem."

B

MANAGE YOUR GLOBAL WRITING

The Case of the Belgian Fries

You're a U.S. businessperson who's just begun negotiations in Antwerp. Your Belgian counterparts have taken you to lunch at an outdoor café. When the food comes—probably mussels and what we call "french fries"—one of them turns to you and says, "Have some of these fries; they're so much better than the terrible fries you have in America!"

How do you respond?

As business becomes more global, more and more businesspeople find themselves communicating internationally. This communication is taking place at all levels of organizations. For example, at one of our client companies, a U.S. insurance firm owned by a five-nation European alliance, nearly 20 percent of all employees reported communicating outside their continent more than once a month, mostly in writing.

This appendix, by Kenneth W. Davis, Teun De Rycker, and J. Piet Verckens, appeared, in an earlier form, as an article in the October 1997 issue of *Global Workforce* magazine.

When businesspeople communicate internationally, they bring to that communication their own communication styles. We suggest that four such styles are prevalent in international business communication. By understanding these four styles, and by recognizing them in ourselves and others, we can all become more effective global communicators, in speech and in writing—and help ourselves and our organizations survive and thrive in the growing world market.

AN INTERNATIONAL COMMUNICATION GRID

In his book *The Seven Habits of Highly Effective People*, Stephen R. Covey argued that all our interactions are colored by the amount of consideration we have for the feelings and convictions of others and by the amount of "courage" we have in embodying our own feelings and convictions. He graphed these two variables against each other in a grid that defines four styles—or "paradigms"—of human interaction.

Covey suggested that in low-consideration, low-courage transactions, both parties lose. By not having the courage of our own feelings and convictions, we don't get what we want, and by not considering the feelings and convictions of others, we're not able to give them what *they* want.

Similarly, low-consideration, high-courage transactions are attempts at "win-lose" bargaining. We say "attempts" because, as Covey argued, one party in an interaction cannot truly win unless the other party wins as well. High-consideration, low-courage transactions, on the other hand, promote a "lose-win" result. Covey's grid shows that "win-win" transactions take place only when we bring a paradigm of both high consideration and high courage.

We have found that these same four styles dominate international business communication. That is, the same grid can be used to define the four main kinds of international business communicators: *isolationist, ugly tourist, gone native,* and *global communicator,* as shown in Figure B-1.

Figure B-1 Four styles of international communication.

High consideration	**Gone native**	**Global communicator**
Low consideration	**Isolationist**	**Ugly tourist**
	Low courage	**High courage**

Four Styles of International Communication

In the lower-left cell of the grid is the *isolationist*. Isolationist communicators bring a low embodiment of their own cultural identity, their own feelings and convictions, and they bring a low consideration for the cultural identities of others. As a result, real communication never takes place.

In the lower-right cell is the *ugly tourist*. The phrase is adapted from the title of William J. Lederer's novel *The Ugly American*. The book's title has become a common phrase for a certain kind of American when traveling overseas, one with a high assertion of his or her own culture but with a low consideration for the host culture—complaining loudly, for example, that "you can't get a good hamburger in Tokyo." However, our phrase *ugly tourist* reflects the fact that such behavior is not restricted to Americans.

Far too many businesspeople fall into this category, strongly asserting their own culture and their own business agenda, but not recognizing the culture or agenda of others. They work hard for a "win," but by not allowing their international partners to win as well, they lose in the long run. They tend to see the world through their own cultural filters without being aware of those filters.

For example, we talked with a Canadian businesswoman who complained that the Dutch with whom she deals answer her questions with too much information. "When I ask what was the 1994 price, I expect to get the 1994 price, no more," she said. However, in the same interview, she called the European belief that North Americans are too literal "not a fair characterization."

In the upper-left cell is the paradigm we call *gone native*. The phrase may have originated in the days of the British Empire to describe the kind of foreign service officer who became so immersed in the local culture that he stopped being of service to the Crown.

The temptation to "go native" always exists for the modern international businessperson as well. In any company, people with international interests tend to be attracted to international positions. Such positions, in any country's corporations, are occupied by more than their share of Anglophiles, Francophiles, "Japanophiles," or "Americophiles." And we've all heard the advice, "When in Rome, do as the Romans do."

This kind of high consideration for others' cultures is desirable in international businesspeople. But when it is coupled, as in this cell of the grid, with low embodiment of one's own culture and one's own interests, the result is a "lose-win" bargain, ultimately no bargain at all.

THE GLOBAL COMMUNICATOR

We suggest, of course, that the most effective paradigm lies in the upper-right cell of the grid. We call this paradigm the *global communicator*, the businessperson who brings high consideration for others' culture but also the high courage of accepting his or her own culture.

We interviewed such a global communicator, a Portuguese businessman working in Amsterdam on the creation of structures for sharing knowledge across a multinational company. This manager clearly asserted his own culture. He seemed proud of being Portuguese as he spoke of his culture's distinctive characteristics. But he also spoke admiringly of the strengths of the other cultures represented in the company.

His high-consideration, high-courage paradigm emerged for us most clearly when we asked if he liked being greeted in Portuguese before switching to English, the working language of his company. "Yes," he said, "it's a nice token gesture. But attitude is more important—to be a joyful person, to be open-minded. And there are other ways to convey that attitude."

USING THE GRID

So back to that Antwerp café and to the challenge: "Have some of these fries; they're so much better than the terrible fries you have in America!" How do you respond? The grid suggests four possible ways.

If you're an *isolationist*, you ignore the challenge and say nothing. Perhaps you change the subject. Conflict is avoided, but communication doesn't happen. The result is lose-lose.

If you're an *ugly tourist*, you rise to the bait. "Are you kidding? You call these fries? In America we wouldn't feed these to a pig." In the right relationship, built over time, a good laugh may follow. But in most cases, the result will be win-lose. You've satisfied your offended honor but lost a chance to build a relationship.

If you've *gone native*, you roll over and play dead. "You're absolutely right," you say. "These are much better than we have in the States." You may have ingratiated yourself with your hosts, but you've probably diminished yourself in their eyes. The lose-win result has no long-term payoff.

But if you're a *global communicator*, you say something like, "Ah, I'm sorry that you haven't found good fries in the United States. Next time you're there, I hope you'll let me take you where you can get some very good ones. Or better yet, I hope you'll let me treat you to some more typically American food. But meanwhile, I certainly enjoy these fries; they're very good indeed!"

The result is win-win. You've shown the courage of your own convictions and a consideration for your hosts' culture. Even more important, you've opened a door to furthering your relationship.

So give the grid a try. Use it to examine your international communication, both spoken and written. With practice, you'll become a global communicator.

C

MANAGE YOUR SPEAKING

O f all the ways to communicate, speaking seems the most feared by the most people. In a survey I conducted of more than a hundred business leaders, they named "speaking to a group" as their biggest communication problem. In fact, speaking received more than twice as many first-place votes as the runner-up problem.

Not all fear is bad, of course. Controlled nervousness, even fear, can give a vital energy, an edge, to a presentation. No speech is worse than that of the speaker who has absolutely no fear, who too obviously regards the presentation as a routine chore to get through. This may well be the cause of the response faced by Manager Fred Barnwall in Figure C-1.

But there's no reason to let speaking remain a number one communication problem for you. You can learn to manage your speaking like you manage your writing—or any other business process. Whether you're giving a formal speech to hundreds of listeners or an informal briefing to two or three, you can become less afraid and more effective by taking charge of your preparation process.

To do so, use the same tools—with slightly different emphasis—that you're learning to use in this course to become a five-stage writer, as shown in Figure C-2.

Figure C-1   Manager Fred Barnwell senses a mood shift among his salespeople.

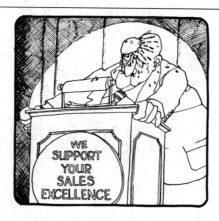

Start by managing, by allocating available time. Then begin a planning stage by "finding the 'we,'" the community to which you and your audience both belong. "PACK" for the journey by asking yourself what personality traits, attitudes, circumstances, and knowledge you and your audience share. Then ask yourself what special personality traits, attitudes, circumstances, and knowledge you have that bring you before this

Figure C-2   Five-stage writing.

audience. Your answers to these questions will help you feel "at home" with your listeners but also qualified to stand before them.

Then "make holes, not drills." Look beyond the speech to the purpose you want it to achieve. Will your presentation function as conversation, correspondence, covenant, or conception for your audience? Start visualizing not the presentation itself but what will happen after it's over. Picture your audience leaving the room filled with new knowledge and new attitudes. Picture them putting your ideas to work in their jobs.

Now start "getting your stuff together," gathering the content of your presentation. Ask the *who, what, where, when, why,* and *how* questions that will lead you to the information you need. Try mind-mapping your content. Remember, however, that a reasonably timed oral presentation has room for *far less* information than a written one. So, for example, instead of the three examples you might use in a report, choose the one best example for your speech.

Then "get your ducks in a row," organizing your material into the best order to achieve your purpose. This step is even more important for speaking than for writing: readers of a badly organized memo or letter can at least skip around to reorganize it in their minds, but listeners to a badly organized speech are stuck with what they're getting. So decide carefully what you want to say first, second, third, and so on.

Now that you've planned your presentation, you're at the main decision point. Will you actually write your speech, or will you speak from notes or an outline? Choose wisely based on your purpose and on the circumstances of the presentation. A written speech is generally appropriate for more formal occasions, of course—but not always. Even if the occasion is relatively informal, written remarks can have great impact, showing you as competent and committed to what you're saying. And a written script, even if you never actually read from it, can help to reduce stage fright by providing "insurance."

If you speak from notes or an outline, tailor them to your needs. Include key words and reminders of key anecdotes or examples. In particular, include reminders of the organization of your presentation so that there's no chance of your getting lost. If you've mind-mapped your speech, consider using your mind map itself as an outline at the podium.

Whether you write your presentation or give it from notes, be sure to emphasize the "turn signals" that let your listeners know where you're going next, as explained in Chapter 7. Transition words and phrases like *therefore, however,* and *next* are even more important in speaking than in writing; your listeners can't look ahead, after all. Also more important in speaking than in writing are "saying what you mean," "paying by the word," and "translating into English," as explained in Chapters 8, 9, and 10. Again, listeners, unlike readers, can't stop to figure out what you mean.

As the Introduction said, information technologies are bringing new importance to the written word. But writing will never completely replace speaking in business or anywhere else. So learn to manage your speaking process. You can become an effective—and almost fearless—speaker.

PRESENTATION GRAPHICS

You've probably heard the quotation from the British Lord Acton, "Power tends to corrupt; absolute power corrupts absolutely." Designer Edward Tufte has changed the quote slightly: "Power corrupts; PowerPoint corrupts absolutely."

That's unfair, of course. Although Microsoft's PowerPoint is the leading presentation graphics program, it's not the only one. But it and its competitors have radically changed the way presentations are prepared and given—not always for the better.

Presentation graphics software has driven us to bullet points as the standard for presentations. Bullet points can seem wonderful for the speaker: they give him or her an easy way to organize a presentation and an easy way not to have to remember it.

That's the problem. Presentation graphics make bad presentations too easy. Not all information should be organized into bullet points. Flip back through this book and notice when I've used bulleted or numbered lists and when I haven't. And bullet points can be boring or distracting to audiences, especially when the speaker simply reads them aloud.

Some of the best presenters today use presentation graphics not for bullet points but for key words or images. (On YouTube, check out presentations by Apple's Steve Jobs or former Vice President Al Gore.) In my most recent presentation, my slides carried only one or two words each, signaling the subtopic I was talking about at each point.

In his blog How to Change the World, visionary thinker Guy Kawasaki offered what he calls the 10-20-30 Rule. Presentations, he said, should have no more than 10 slides. They should last no longer than 20 minutes. They should use no smaller than 30-point fonts.

Give it a try.

A P P P E N D I X

RESOURCES FOR MANAGING YOUR WRITING

BOOKS ON COMMUNICATION IN BUSINESS

Several recent popular books stress the growing importance of communication in business. Among the best are these:

- *The Brand You 50,* by Tom Peters. This small book, one of a trilogy called Reinventing Work, offers 50 tools for becoming a "brand," whether as an entrepreneur or as an employee.
- *The Cluetrain Manifesto: The End of Business as Usual,* by Rick Levine, Christopher Locke, Doc Searls, and David Weinberger. Born on a website, this book signals what I predict will eventually be seen as the biggest change in the history of business communication—the change brought about by computer and Internet use and discussed, in connection with this book, in Appendix A.
- *Good Business: Leadership, Flow, and the Making of Meaning,* by Mihaly Csikszentmihalyi. The psychologist who gave us the "flow" model discussed in Chapter 5 applies that model broadly to the leadership of organizations.

- *The Laws of Simplicity: Design, Technology, Business, Life*, by John Maeda. A quick, hundred-page read, this book presents 10 laws and 3 keys to simplicity, all of which can be applied to business writing.
- *Leading Out Loud: Inspiring Change Through Authentic Communication*, by Terry Pearce. A leading executive coach presents a remarkably deep and broad discussion of leading through communicating with integrity.
- *Made to Stick: Why Some Ideas Survive and Others Die*, by Chip Heath and Dan Heath. This book takes a fresh look, with hundreds of examples, at getting ideas to "stick" through better communication. At least one university has adopted *Made to Stick* and the book you're reading as the two textbooks for a business communication course. They complement each other well.
- *What to Say to Get What You Want*, by Sam Deep and Lyle Sussman. Almost all business communication guides give the "how" of speaking and writing. This book gives the "what" by portraying 44 types of bosses, employees, coworkers, and customers and advising readers on what to say to each.

DICTIONARIES

Be careful when you choose a dictionary: Small paperbacks generally aren't complete enough for business writers, and many hardback dictionaries are out of date or badly edited—even many that carry the name *Webster's*, which isn't a trademark. Fortunately, several reliable hardback desk dictionaries are available. I recommend the following:

- *The American Heritage Dictionary of the English Language.* The most attractive and readable of the major dictionaries, with particular strengths in word histories and usage.
- *Merriam-Webster's Collegiate Dictionary.* The most widely used desk dictionary.

THESAURUSES

Using a thesaurus is risky. It can help you find a word you know but have forgotten. However, it can hurt you by suggesting a word that isn't appropriate or effective for your specific need. My favorites are these:

- *The American Heritage College Thesaurus*
- *Bartlett's Roget's Thesaurus*

USAGE GUIDES

Usage guides cover the etiquette of language from when you can split infinitives to whether you can say *prioritize*. Of the many usage guides available, I recommend:

- *Merriam-Webster's Dictionary of English Usage*

WRITING GUIDES

Surely no book on writing has been more recommended than "Strunk and White." Some of its reputation is undeserved: *The Elements of Style* too often leans toward academic stuffiness and away from practicality. For example, a William Faulkner sentence containing the words *gutful*, *mendicant*, and *thrall* is described as using "ordinary" words. The book is saved, however, by its solid advice and engaging style. It makes for enjoyable reading, with some learning in the process. But several more useful options are available, especially as supplements to this *36-Hour Course*:

- *The Business Writer's Handbook*, by Gerald J. Alred, Charles T. Brusaw, and Walter E. Oliu. This A–Z reference book can answer lots of specific questions at each step in the writing process.
- *The Elements of Business Writing: A Guide to Writing Clear, Concise Letters, Memos, Reports, Proposals, and Other Business Docu-*

ments, by Gary Blake and Robert W. Bly. This book, with an obvious nod to Strunk and White, lists 67 principles of good writing, with about two pages each of details and examples.

- *Revising Business Prose*, by Richard Lanham. Taking the same basic approach to revision as I do, this book has gained wide recognition for its "paramedic method" of revising.
- *The Writing Coach*, by Lee Clark Johns. This large-format book, by a leading writing consultant, is dedicated "to everyone who 'writes for a living'—which means almost all working adults."

OTHER BOOKS

Two other books, though not directly focused on writing, present two of the most useful sets of tools I use as a business writer:

- *Getting Things Done: The Art of Stress-Free Productivity*, by David Allen. Allen's book, the source for the "law of the next action" in my book's introduction, has been invaluable in helping me learn to manage my writing—and much of the rest of my life.
- *The Mind Map Book*, by Tony Buzan with Barry Buzan. Written by the great popularizer of mind-mapping, this beautifully illustrated book is still the best introduction to the subject.

WEB RESOURCES

Because Web pages come and go often, I will not list any here. However, you can find an up-to-date list of recommended links at manage yourwriting.com.

INDEX

233

ABOUT THE AUTHOR

Dr. Kenneth W. Davis is professor emeritus and former chair of English at Indiana University–Purdue University Indianapolis.

With more than 35 years' experience as a business writer, editor, and trainer, Ken has served as director at large of the Association for Business Communication and is immediate past president of the Association of Professional Communication Consultants. Ken's consulting clients have included the Abu Dhabi National Oil Company, the Republic of Botswana, IBM, the International Monetary Fund, and the U.S. Social Security Administration.

Through speaking, training, and executive coaching, Ken helps people and organizations improve their chief value-producing activity: writing. Thousands of knowledge workers have profited from Ken's unique Manage Your Writing® method. This method is the basis for Ken's latest book, *The McGraw-Hill 36-Hour Course in Business Writing and Communication*, which has been translated into Mandarin and is now in its second English-language edition.

Ken lives in Rio Rancho, New Mexico, with his wife and business partner, Bette Davis.

For more information, visit manageyourwriting.com.